THE CHILD DEVELOPMENT PROGRAM:

Preventing and Remediating Learning Problems

Suzanne Sosna Levine

Baywood Publishing Company, Inc.
AMITYVILLE, NEW YORK

Library of Congress Catalog Number: 96-28755
ISBN: 0-89503-144-2 (pbk.)

Library of Congress Cataloging-in-Publication Data

Levine, Suzanne Sosna.
    The child development program : preventing and remediating learning problems / Suzanne Sosna Levine.
        p.   cm.
    Includes bibliographical references and index.
    ISBN 0-89503-144-2 (pbk.)
    1. Learning disabled children- -Education (Elementary)- -United States. 2. Remedial teaching- -United States. 3. Learning disabilities- -Treatment- -United States. 4. Child development- -United States. 5. Readiness for school- -United States. I. Title.
    LC4705.L483   1996   96-28755
    371.91- -dc20   CIP

Appendix to The Child Development Program: ISBN 0-89503-145-0
2-Volume Set: ISBN 0-89503-146-9

Dedication

This book is dedicated to the thousands of children who have been more successful because they participated in the Child Development Program, as well as to the millions, hopefully, who will be helped to achieve more, academically and in all ways through the dissemination of information by its publication and distribution.

Foreword

I am fortunate to be the wife of developmental optometrist Dr. Stanley H. Levine. In the early sixties, his work with children who had visually-related learning problems influenced my choice of a post-motherhood career. Having taught four years in grades one and two early in our marriage, I knew there were some students I had not reached through regular teaching methods. Witnessing the positive changes in children brought about by the various exercises being done in my husband's office, I saw the feasibility of borrowing some of these techniques to use in the classroom.

As the youngest of our three daughters entered nursery school, I returned to college for a master's degree in special education. Luck smiled on me once more, when, as a federal fellowship recipient, I was assigned to work at the Newark State (now Kean) College Evaluation Clinic with psychologist Jay Roth. Dr. Roth was also on the staff of North Brunswick, New Jersey, Public Schools. The Child Development Program which Dr. Roth had designed was in its infancy, and when he asked if I would be interested in working with children who had mild perceptual problems, I was pleased to join this innovative group.

Early in my involvement with the Child Development Program, I knew that it was effective and needed to be shared. An article that I wrote about it was published in a national teachers' magazine and drew many responses asking for more information. This book is my way of giving these helpful techniques to all who are interested in assisting children to develop to their full potential.

Acknowledgments

Acknowledgments

It is with deep gratitude that I acknowledge the contributions of developmental (or behavioral) optometry to the work done in the Child Development Program. On behalf of all the children (and adults) who are more successful because of the work they did with guidance from *Developing Learning Readiness,* I wish to thank the authors: G. N. Getman, O.D., Marvin R. Halgren, O.D., Elmer R. Kane, Ed.D., and Gordon W. McKee, O.D., who made it possible. My sincere thanks are herewith extended to Mrs. Clara Getman and the Optometric Extension Program Foundation, Inc. for permission to reprint *Developing Learning Readiness*.

Thanks, also, to Arthur C. Heinsen, O.D., for permission to reprint parts of *Visual Motor Development*.

Thanks to Maury Leon of Book-Lab, Inc. for permission to include a copy of the Cursive Writing paper which has proven to be a valuable aide in the Child Development Program's Handwriting Clinics.

My appreciation is also extended to Educational Developmental Laboratories, Inc. of Columbia, South Carolina, for permission to reproduce parts of their *Look and Write* workbook which is no longer in print.

Thanks to Andrew J. Costello, who, as principal of John Adams School in North Brunswick, New Jersey, was supportive and encouraging. His criticism was always constructive, and he shared my enthusiasm when each of our Child Development students graduated from the Program. Most important, it was he who encouraged me to work on the preventive aspect of the Program, while maintaining the remedial.

I acknowledge my debt to Louise Bates Ames, psychologist, associate director of Gesell Institute of Human Development, New Haven, Connecticut, and author of *Is Your Child in the Wrong Grade?* and *Don't Push Your Preschooler* along with other books which have not only reinforced my opinion, but have helped many parents to make the right decisions regarding their children.

Finally, my thanks for many years of cooperative effort to Jimmie Mast and all the other teachers through the years who worked with the children we loved.

Table of Contents

Introduction

The Child Development Program was designed to be an immediate intervention, working with children in the early elementary grades who are having difficulty accomplishing what their classmates are doing with relative ease. As presented in this book, this Program currently is found only in North Brunswick, New Jersey. The work described is from my experience as the Child Development teacher in John Adams School from 1968 to 1992. Any opinions stated or implied are my own and not necessarily those of the Board of Education of North Brunswick, New Jersey.

While many readers of this book are or will be educators, some are from other disciplines such as psychology, optometry, physical therapy, occupational therapy, as well as simply interested parents. For this reason, I have tried to keep the vocabulary as specific, yet comprehensible as possible. It is my way of helping the largest number of adults to help the largest number of children.

Although in my experience more boys than girls have been participants in the Child Development Program, the use of "he" or "she" can be interchanged in the general descriptions of children in this book.

Developing Learning Readiness and the *Clymer-Barrett Prereading Battery*, which have been out-of-print for years now appear in the Appendix to this book. Some modifications had to be made to replace the filmstrips which accompanied the former.

As you read Chapters 1 and 2 you will become acquainted with the preventive aspect of the Child Development Program, as well as some of the developmental efforts undertaken with specific individuals at the Kindergarten level, when needed.

Chapter 3 describes the beginning of the review and reinforcement work done in grade one to promote a more successful foundation in the basic areas of reading, printing, and arithmetic. The procedures suggested are still of a developmental nature, and emphasis is placed on the visual, motor, and auditory skills that are required to affect learning.

Beyond grade one, if problems are still encountered in producing what the teacher is requesting, there is usually some form of perceptual and/or motor difficulty, many of which can be remedied with training. It was in response to this challenge that psychologist Jay Roth designed the Child Development Program. Chapter 4 presents his analysis of the problem, the premise of his efforts, and the description of the implementation of the Program from the plan to the practice.

Chapter 5 suggests several basic improvements, some of which have been gleaned from other areas such as physiology, optometry, nutrition, and psychology. Once the importance of these interventions is recognized by educators (including administrators), the big winners will be the children.

Chapter 6 discusses the development of motor and visual skills. There is some overlapping, since most motor skills are visually directed if they are to be purposeful.

The auditory skills as they impact on learning, and how to develop them is addressed in Chapter 7.

Over the years, we have used various commercially available programs for supplemental or remedial instruction in the basic curriculum areas of math, reading, and writing, once we have eliminated the perceptual roadblocks. Chapter 8 gives a brief review of our favorites.

The technical side of organizing a Child Development Program in your school district and keeping it running efficiently is addressed in Chapter 9.

Four detailed case histories are presented in Chapter 10. The children described were very different in their needs and in the length of their participation in the Program.

One of the children who came back into my life as an adult wrote Chapter 11 describing his feelings in John Adams School and the Child Development Program, as he recalls them, and how they shaped his life.

Chapter 12 gives the reader a brief historical picture of the Child Development Program, how it remained flexible enough to expand its coverage without losing its basic goals and its identity.

Chapter 13 "Sources" lists all of the items mentioned and where they may be obtained.

If you find the preceding material interesting, you may want to continue broadening your horizons by reading the books listed in Chapter 14.

CHAPTER 1

Pre-Kindergarten Screening

Surprises are fun when they are parties or presents, but when you are a kindergarten teacher, it helps to know before school begins if any of your students has a problem. It gives you a chance to prepare whatever you might need, depending on the child's specific problem. Once you have witnessed what can happen in a kindergarten class when a child has a separation-from-Mommy problem (I'll never forget the frightened little boy whom I had to carry off the school bus, kicking and screaming, into the kindergarten classroom only to have him sink his teeth into my arm as I tried to release him to the teacher) or a developmental lag which prevents him from being able to do everything that his peers can do, you appreciate the idea of a little getting acquainted session prior to the beginning of school.

At John Adams School in North Brunswick, New Jersey, every spring we invite each kindergarten registrant to come with a parent and spend a half-hour with the Child Development Teacher. When we started this in 1975, we made up our own screening instrument. Based on *Performance Objectives for Preschool Children,* [1] it gave us some insight into each child's development with regard to visual, motor, cognitive, language, and social skills. Now we use the BRIGANCE®[1] K & 1 Screen, which is standardized and simple to administer.

Each year in March, we have our Kindergarten Roundup: the community is advised through the media and fliers sent home with students to come on a specified day and register their children who will be five years old by September 1. (The cut-off date was December 31 until about 5 years ago.) Each youngster is given an appointment with a reminder notice to color and bring back on a day in May. A letter of explanation from the head of Special Services allays any possible parental anxieties, and we usually get excellent cooperation.

Parent and child arrive at the scheduled time and are directed to the Child Development room by a colorful poster in the school's front lobby. After a minute or two of introductions, the parent is seated in the same room and the child is engaged in a little game of bouncing an 8-1/2″ playground ball. Part of the screening assesses gross-motor development which requires the child to perform a series of physical activities demonstrated by the teacher, such as hopping, balancing, walking heel-to-toe, etc. By the time we have finished this, the child is warming up to the whole situation. Then we settle down at a little table where the parent can watch the child's responses, but the child cannot watch the parent's face, and continue to gather information. How the child responds to the simple question, "How old are you?" can tell us how mature he is. If the answer is silently, four fingers held up in the air, this indicates "not very," as compared with another who replies crisply, "I'm four-and-a-half years old." Does he know his address? His birthday? Can he recognize likenesses and differences?

---

[1] BRIGANCE® is a registered trademark of Curriculum Associates, Inc.

For example, when shown a page of ten long rectangles, each containing four shapes or letters, can the child point to the one on each line that is different from the other three? The sample has three cats and a bird. The next row has a circle and three squares. The task gets progressively more difficult, but still achievable by most four- to five-year-olds, with three x's and a y in the final group.

When the youngster is given a pencil, blank paper, and the task to copy some designs from the book, we are looking at the way he holds his pencil, the distance he keeps between his eyes and the paper as well as how accurately he can replicate the circle, horizontal line, cross, square, and triangle. If his pencil grip is awkward, we note it. At the end of the session, we will demonstrate the correct grip, forming a triangle around the pencil with thumb, pointer, and middle finger, about one-inch up from the tip. We use Try-Rex® pencils which are three-sided, but if he seems to need more help with this, we'll even give him a little plastic device that fits on any pencil to take home in order to reinforce the correction. If he's been holding his head closer than twelve inches from the paper consistently while drawing, or has been tilting his head to one side or covering one eye while looking at the tasks presented, we will advise having his vision checked by the family optometrist.

While our pre-kindergartener has been responding to our questions, we have also noticed his speech and language development. If there are any apparent problems in this area, we make note of it for follow-up by the speech teacher or, if more appropriate, by the teacher of our English-as-a-Second Language program.

There are still more areas assessed by the BRIGANCE® K & 1 Screen: Can he recognize and correctly name the ten basic colors? Numerals? Letters? Does he understand number concepts? When you direct his attention to the numerals from 1 to 5, can he match the correct number of fingers to each, even if they are not in numerical order? Can he show you where his elbow, ankle, hip, wrist, heel, waist, shoulder, chin, fingernails, and jaw are? Can he print his first name?

The successful response to each of these items carries a score. When totaled, if the child has fewer than 65 points, we are concerned that he may have problems in our kindergarten. Here is where intervention often begins to help. If he has had no nursery school experience, and perhaps has not been stimulated by an enriching home situation, it's entirely possible that his BRIGANCE® score could be low.

Immediately following the session with Junior, we review the findings with Mom or Dad and give suggestions of things they can do at home to enhance their child's ability to perform the various tasks with which he had trouble. Simply going over the names of the letters and numbers, with some suggestions for making this into a game at home can start the family on a new adventure together. Sometimes we get the response, "I thought that's what they're supposed to learn at school!" Then we need to explain that because so many of our children have already had more than a year of nursery school, we have developed a rather academically advanced curriculum in our kindergarten. Often, in fact, our children learn to read before they enter first grade.

We find it helps to hand the parents a sheet with all the letters, both capitals and lower-case, advising that they cover it with clear Contact® paper and mount it on the front of their refrigerator, low enough so that Junior can trace them with his finger, following the tiny arrows directing the correct formation (see Figure 1). A second page with the numerals from 1 to 10 is also given (see Figure 2). By teaching the right way from the beginning, we

Figure 1.

USING NUMERALS

Dear Parents,

We are learning to recognize and use numerals. You can help us enjoy learning the many uses of numerals and how to write them.

At school we have discovered that each numeral has a name and that it is written in many ways. We do not expect to find it the same way all the time, but we write it the same way each time we use it at school.

On this page are examples of the way we write numerals. Practice writing them in this way so that you can use them when you are writing with your child. Keep the examples for your child to use as models when he begins to do his own writing.

Play games and have fun with numerals as your child discovers them everywhere. Some suggestions follow.

1. Take a walk and read the numerals on house numbers, street numbers, license plates, and other places you find.

2. Find numerals that are alike on a newspaper page such as a grocery advertisement—the 9's, 5's, 2's, etc.

3. Find the same numeral in different places at home, such as clock, television dial, page number.

Sincerely,

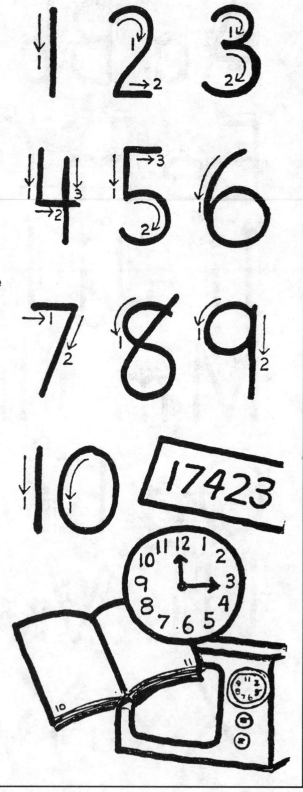

Figure 2.

find there is less need for correcting and reteaching later on. There is less confusion on the part of the learner and fewer chances for reversals to occur.

Another thing we never take for granted is how the child holds a scissor. By giving him a cutting task and the choice of right- or left-handed scissors, we can determine not only how skillful he is, but also how much effort he had to exert. The correct way to hold a scissor is with the thumb through the top hole, the middle finger through the bottom hole, and the index finger curved under the bottom blade. This gives the most control to the cutter, and gets the task done with a minimum of effort and frustration.

Occasionally we find a child who is developmentally lagging behind his chronological peers. For whatever reason, and there are many, this child will be the one who has no desire to cooperate in this get-acquainted situation. He may show his immaturity by climbing up into mother's lap or hiding under the table. He may refuse to respond verbally, or may just act silly. His mother might shrug with a smile and offer further information such as, "He doesn't like to sit and listen to stories," or "I can't get him to do anything with a pencil and paper." Here we have a choice to offer: first, if we suspect a significant developmental problem severe enough to require special education even at this level, we would suggest that the child be evaluated by our Special Services Child Study Team. Second, we can recommend that the child attend our pre-kindergarten summer program which runs three hours daily for four weeks in July, followed by another parent-teacher conference to decide on his readiness for kindergarten in September. In either case, we have the advantage of getting another professional viewpoint to help determine the best placement for the child, and the parent is usually willing to cooperate.

If this sounds like a lot of work, it is. It also pays tremendous dividends in the smooth beginning of school for all involved. The data-filled BRIGANCE® score sheets, with the extra pages showing each child's cutting, copying, printing of name, and a self-portrait drawn while the Child Development teacher is conferring with the parent are placed in folders, and presented to the kindergarten teachers, set up in classes for September usually on the last day of school. If there are any potential learning problems coming in, they've already been flagged and the proper staff notified, i.e., the Summer School Director or Special Services staff. In either case, a short report has been prepared by the Child Development teacher highlighting the concerns regarding each child who might be considered "at risk" of having learning problems.

This procedure has been followed annually since 1975, with minor variations, and both Special Services and the kindergarten teachers have found it extremely helpful. It gives us all an introduction to each child, puts the child at ease, develops excellent rapport with the parents, and allows all involved to get to work on the first day of school, with no tears and no unwanted surprises.

REFERENCE

1. G. J. Schirmer, editor, *Performance Objectives for Preschool Children*, Adapt Press, Inc., Sioux Falls, South Dakota, 1974.

CHAPTER 2

Kindergarten—The Child Development Perspective

With such detailed preparation done in the spring of each year, the first day of school in September is usually busy and productive. The new kindergarteners are settling in, making friends, learning to share the teacher's attention as well as sharing the puzzles, blocks, and floor space. The Child Development and Reading teachers turn their efforts toward any late-enrolling newcomers, usually people who have moved in during the summer. It sometimes takes a few days to complete the screening of the upper grade students for math and reading levels.

Since both of the developmental programs employed by the Child Development teacher in kindergarten are best when used before formal printing lessons begin, we like to start them by the second week of school. *Developing Learning Readiness,* [1] has been in use in the kindergarten at John Adams School in North Brunswick, New Jersey, since 1973. It is a visual-motor-tactile skills program consisting of a series of sequentially organized exercises designed to be used with pre-school and elementary school children and is also helpful in special education classrooms. The teacher's manual found in the Appendix provides the rationale and purpose of each set of activities, along with illustrations and very detailed instructions.

The question might be raised at this point: Why? Why do we need to give every kindergartener all these exercises? The answer, perhaps over-simplified, is that in our society with so much sedentary activity (television and video games), many children have not had the opportunity to develop the prerequisite skills for formal learning by the time they reach first grade. As developmental optometrist, A. J. Kirshner concluded after thirty years of clinical experience:

> I have had rich experiences in helping children because I have given priority to the sensorimotor status of the child and have tried to make the curriculum relevant. Opening the channels of communication by sensory training, developing the responsive functions of the organism through skilled movement, and finally, integrating all the sense modalities through rhythmic movement patterns visually directed, will not only increase the effectiveness of children who are not meeting the demands of daily life, but will enhance and enrich the lives of children who are meeting the standards set by the community [2, p. 88].

Research done by Getman, Kane, Halgren, McKee, Kirshner, and many others in the field has proven that children who have used this program are much more successful in their future academic work than those who have not been given the training, even though all had comparable intellectual ability.[1]

Starting with practice in general coordination, we move on through exercises in balance, using a walking beam to develop among other skills, peripheral awareness. The next sequence enhances eye-hand coordination, also increasing attention span for visual activities. Triple-thickness chalk and a chalkboard are used with these activities. The next step is eye movement exercises which help each child develop the control and accuracy of eye movements required in learning tasks such as shifting from near to far targets and back to near. Think of how often in school a child is required to look at the chalkboard, then down to his desk and up to the board again. With the exercises given in *Developing Learning Readiness*, the eyes are trained to perform this activity with ease and accuracy. Smooth saccades (side-to-side sweeps) are also taught to enable the child to scan a line and select the important item from among many. Form recognition is next in the series and develops integration of eye-hand actions and visual-tactile information. Templates of basic shapes are utilized during this portion of the program. The visual-memory segment is the final one of the series.

When used as directed in the manual, *Developing Learning Readiness* has proven its ability to do that consistently, and the children enjoy it. They look forward to the sessions and cooperate with the teachers throughout. They advance in small enough increments to feel successful at every level. Out of print for many years, a slightly revised version appears in the Appendix to this book.

"Perception +"[2] is a series of forty cardboard visuals, along with a teacher's guide giving very specific directions for administration. These should be read carefully before working with the students. Teachers must be made aware of the unique qualities of this program because the success of "Perception +" depends to a large degree on the teacher's restraint. Rather than being taught by the teacher, children are encouraged to observe and learn through their own discoveries as well as those of their classmates.

Each of the lessons consists of three separate activities: 1) visual analysis with verbal description, 2) relating the abstract to the real, and 3) the graphic replication of the instructional models.

Each of the visuals, sequenced in progressive degree of difficulty, is printed in orange enclosed by a black frame of reference. The children, grouped in front of it so that all can get an unobstructed view, are given the word "frame" as a starting point. The first board we present shows a black rectangle, 9″ × 12″, set length-wise on a white 12″ × 15″ card. We ask the children to tell us about the frame. Only a few need to respond at each session. The first lesson might sound something like this:

> Teacher: Children, this is a frame. What can you tell me about this frame?
> Child #1: It looks like a box.

---

[1] Research based on experimental use in Golden Valley School District, Minneapolis, of the program in 1963, when it was known as *The Physiology of Readiness*.

[2] "Perception +," known originally as Project:SEE (Specific Education of the Eye) started as a Title III effort under the joint cooperation of the Union Township, New Jersey Board of Education and the Office of Program Development, Division of Research, Planning and Evaluation, New Jersey State Department of Education, 1972. It was designed by Milton Knobler, then head of the Union Township Art Department. For information on ordering, please see "Sources."

Child #2: It looks like a rectangle.

Child #3: It's black.

Teacher: Very good! What do you see in this frame?

Child #4: Nothing.

Teacher: Yes, this is an empty frame, but let's just make sure everyone knows what this part of the frame is called, (pointing to the top).

Child #5: That's the top.

Teacher: Then this must be . . . (pointing to the bottom).

Child #6: The bottom.

The sides must be differentiated: "Left side" and "Right side." We might take one more minute to reinforce this by having a child come forward and have him place his left hand on the left side and his right hand on the right side as he stands facing the frame.

"Now, children, in the next frame, you will see something, and I want you to tell us about it," we continue. We now display card #1, which shows one horizontal orange line about one-third up from the bottom of the frame. Calling on children to talk about it, we might hear, "I see an orange line." "What else can you tell us, Sally?" "It's a straight line." "Is this line touching anything, Bobby?" "Yes, it's touching the sides of the frame." "Okay, now, look carefully. Is the line closer to the bottom or to the top of the frame?" "It's closer to the bottom!" proclaims Billy. "Good for all of you! Now look around the room and see if you can find another line that looks something like this one." "Up there," comes one reply, as Christine points to the top of the bulletin board. "There's one," says Sally, pointing to the chalk tray. "And here's one in front of the window!" discovers Bobby.

"Wonderful! We're really wide awake today! Now each of you will get a paper that has an empty frame on it. Look here once more (pointing to the visual) and then you try to make a line with your pencil in your frame that looks just like this straight orange line in my frame."

The teacher then circulates throughout the group giving a few seconds to each child, evaluating performance, rewarding good efforts with a little smiling face. If a child has drawn the line too close to the top, we bring the visual to the child, have him measure with fingers to see how to replicate it more accurately, and give him a second try. If no one has used the word yet, we might wind up the lesson this way: "Today you've learned to do a grown-up thing: you can recognize and make a horizontal line! Say that big word with me: HOR-I-ZON-TAL." The first lesson is over.

Lesson #2 is a vertical line closer to the left than to the right. Lesson #3 is an oblique line starting near the top right and going toward bottom center. Lesson #4 is a half-circle open at the bottom. Following four presentations, a larger sheet (legal size paper) with four smaller empty frames is distributed for a review lesson. At that time, we simply display the visuals, one at a time, without discussion, indicating only in which frame the children are to replicate each design.

When we first started these programs in our kindergartens, we only had *Developing Learning Readiness*. Because we could accommodate only one-half of the class on the floor at one time, we divided the children into two groups. The Child Development teacher would work with one group while the other group did some activity at their tables with the kindergarten teacher. After about seven or eight minutes, we would switch groups. We found that fifteen minutes was sufficient for each lesson with the whole class. When we initiated

"Perception +" in 1974, one of us would do that with half the class while the other did *Developing Learning Readiness* with the other half. Then we'd switch groups, so all the children got both full lessons. The best scheduling for us has been three times per week, but we have found that even twice a week is worthwhile. Probably in a full-day kindergarten situation, we would use both programs daily because the children enjoy them so much and benefit from them so dramatically.

Over the years, we have found that most of the children who have experienced these programs in kindergarten have done well in all their schoolwork, with good eye-hand skills and well-developed vocabularies. They have become competent readers and can copy from board or book with few, if any, errors. Usually, they can attend to lessons for longer periods of time without losing their concentration, and, in general, are more successful than those students who moved in from other districts where these developmental programs were not available. On an investment of forty-five minutes (15 minutes, Monday, Wednesday, and Friday) per week, per kindergarten class, we have reaped a rich harvest that cannot be measured merely in money or time.

Sometimes there will be a few children who don't get enough in those forty-five minutes per week to make up for lack of stimulation or too minimal parental guidance during the important first five years of life. There will also be some who may have a developmental deficiency. These are the children we may have noted during the pre-kindergarten screening, so we know that extra input is needed. Depending on the extent of their difficulties, we already may have started to work with them one-to-one or in a small group. We may start with these youngsters in their classroom, right at their side, helping them follow the directions being given by their teacher. If this method doesn't produce a more successful student within a trial period of a few weeks, we may need to take the youngster out to the Child Development room for more in-depth work, strengthening whatever weaknesses are impeding the child's progress, and alerting the parents to our specific concerns.

We usually start some diagnostic testing at this point to pinpoint the problem areas. First, we have the school nurse check the child's sight and hearing. Both of these are routine screenings in public schools in North Brunswick, and are done periodically with each class. At the beginning of kindergarten, the nurse may not have screened this group yet. Once we are assured that the problem is not in either of these information-gathering areas, we may proceed to use other tests to determine where in the processing of information the child's difficulty exists.

Most recently, we've been using the *Test of Visual-Perceptual Skills (nonmotor)*, the *Test of Visual-Motor Skills,* and *Test of Auditory-Perceptual Skills*. Each of these is individually administered and yields considerable information over and above the scores achieved by the student. The way a child responds to each test can be very enlightening. Does Johnny look at each of the multiple choice answers before selecting one? Or does he almost randomly point to an answer while searching the examiner's face for approval. For this reason, one must learn to keep a pleasantly neutral expression while testing. Does Jane respond to questions verbally or does she merely point to her choice? Perhaps she isn't sure of the number names yet, or is she just very shy? When Tommy taps his answer, he does so several times, rapidly, in a perseverative manner. Could this possibly indicate neurological involvement? An alert examiner notes such observations on the test for future discussion, if needed, with the Special Services Child Study Team. One must also be alert to the child's limit for sitting and attending to a task. The child of five or six should not be expected to work for longer than ten to fifteen minutes at one job if we are interested in getting the best he has to offer.

We consider it important to establish rapport with parents. At the beginning of each child's introduction to school, we met with at least one parent at the Pre-K Screening. We usually meet again at a Kindergarten Orientation for Parents on the second Friday afternoon in June. It is standard procedure for us to contact parents to inform them that we are doing some testing which will help us to help their child. We've told them earlier that we consider parents the first and most important teachers in their child's life. We have Open School Night each September to enable all of the parents to come and meet their children's teachers. While sitting in their child's seat, an overview of the curriculum for the year is presented. The Child Development teacher is also available that evening to explain briefly the intent and content of this program.

Following the perceptual skills testing, we have a conference with the parents, preferably in school or, if need be, on the phone. At this time we review first what the problem appears to be. The kindergarten teacher has already been in touch with the parents about it. Then we review the tests we have used to determine the child's functioning ability and finally, our plan for improvement. Each child is different. Each set of responses is different. Yet, over time, enough similarities arise with which to base a plan for action. The Child Development Program is very pragmatic in its attitude toward helping children. We will try one set of exercises, and if it doesn't work, we'll try a different set. The things that work for one child may not work for another. The activities that work the best are the ones we tend to use first and most regularly.

Suppose Jimmy has demonstrated a visual-motor problem which is hindering his ability to copy accurately from the chalkboard. He cannot stay on the correct line and it takes him too long to complete the task, which is full of errors after all his hard work anyway. We outline briefly some of the exercises we can use to develop the skills Jimmy has not developed on his own, as listed in Chapter 6. There are games and activities he could play at home that would also help, and the parents are encouraged to be team members in working toward their child's success. Most parents are willing, in fact, eager to help, and we guide them.

Whatever the testing indicated as "areas of need," we will address with a wide variety of techniques. By changing the developmental/remedial activities frequently, we keep the child's interest and motivation high.

In order to schedule the child to do these various activities, we need to meet with the kindergarten teacher and let her know everything we have told the parents plus the time slot we would like to have the child. This will vary depending on the severity and extent of the problem, and whether there are any others in the class with the same difficulty. Suppose only Jimmy is exhibiting this particular need, and it is rather severe: he cannot get his work done independently, while all his classmates are sailing right along. We might ask that Jimmy be excused from his classroom for fifteen minutes every morning to have him come to the Child Development room where we will do as many as three or four training activities daily. Very important to this child's welfare is that he not miss any instructional time from his class. The teacher will check her schedule and give the Child Development teacher a time slot, perhaps when the other children are doing "independent" activities. If there are two students with similar difficulties, we might want to take them together for twenty minutes.

We begin to work with the child (or children) using their strengths to reach their weaknesses, and keeping the daily sessions light and as interesting as possible. If we have already completed the two developmental programs, and Jimmy is still having trouble keeping up with the rest of the class, we might start him on *Visual Motor Development* [3]. He will practice controlling his eye movements even more specifically than before (see Figure 1). He will need to follow a moving target visually (see Figure 2) and learn to "read" a page of pictures of pigs and ducks, saying "Oink" or "Quack" when each is the appropriate response (see Figure 3). Once he has mastered that task, he will do it in rhythm, that will encourage his eyes to move at a steady pace across the page. Gradually, we increase the difficulty by adding arrows pointing up, down, left, and right (see Figure 4). The third level mixes pigs, ducks, and arrows, still with a steady tapping to keep the beat (we use an electronic metronome) (see Figure 5). The fourth and final challenge of this particular series is to read pigs, ducks, arrows, and blank spaces, giving each blank space the same time value as the symbols (see Figure 6). The children love this program, and really enjoy doing this for homework.

Usually, by the end of these series of exercises, along with practice in the actual use of the pencil and crayon (yes, there really are some children who have never held one of these before kindergarten), and practice doing the assignments that had been causing the difficulties originally, the child is ready to "graduate" from the Child Development Program.

If, after all the procedures in our repertoire are exhausted, the child is still not meeting with success regularly and independently, we suggest to the parents that they see a developmental (sometimes called "behavioral") optometrist. We offer a list of five or six such specialists who have the credentials and expertise, explaining that the school cannot be responsible for providing these services. These vision specialists have had postgraduate training in children's vision problems, as well as years of clinical experience and their names are available from at least two sources:

> College of Optometrists in Vision Development
> P. O. Box 285
> Chula Vista, CA 92010

and

> Optometric Extension Program Foundation, Inc.
> 1921 East Carnegie Ave., Suite 3-L
> Santa Ana, CA 92705-5510

Occasionally, we find a child who needs their special help, and parents come back to thank us for our assistance in locating the proper professionals.

Before leaving kindergarten, our children need to have learned all the numbers and letters, and how to put them to use. Simple addition and subtraction, as well as simple phonetically regular words (cat, sat, mat, etc.) plus enough "sight" words (the, was, of, etc.) to be able to read on a pre-primer level are all prerequisites for our first grades. If the children we have been helping have not yet achieved this cognitive level, we need to help them do that, too. Through the use of special programs such as Structural Arithmetic, the Cove School Reading Program, Primary Phonics, and others listed in Chapter 8, we continue to teach and then to review the very basic foundation of academics.

head versions

purpose   To establish the correct correlation of activity between the eye muscles and the neck muscles, and to increase the child's awareness of his position in space.

equipment   A full-length mirror and a balance board. Note: This procedure may be carried out without the mirror and/or the balance board if they are unavailable.

set up (using mirror)   Have the child stand three to five feet from the mirror, facing it. His feet should be slightly apart; his hands at his sides.

procedure **1** Looking steadily at his eyes in the mirror, the child alternates moving his head in each of three directions: A "yes" movement, a "no" movement and a tilt movement. The tilt movement is made as if there were a horizontal axis running through the child's neck, from front to back. The tilt activity is the most difficult, and should be done with minimal movement of the chin.

      2 It is essential that the child maintain fixation upon his own eyes in the mirror while making all of these movements. He should carry the movements to their extreme limits, stretching his neck muscles as far as possible, at the same time avoiding body movements. The movements should be smooth, rhythmic, and coordinated. As the movements do become smooth and rhythmic, the child should be reminded to become increasingly aware of the visual world surrounding him.

Figure 1. **Source:** See [3]. Reprinted with permission.

3   As the child becomes adept in his movements, you may ask him to carry out these activities while maintaining balance on the balance board. As the balance board is intended to increase, or "load" the challenge, it should be used only with those children who are experiencing no difficulty in the basic procedure.

4   **Head versions** should be practiced for approximately five minutes per training session.

**set up
(without mirror)**   Arrange the children into partner teams of approximately equal height, and have them look into each other's eyes.

procedure   The children take turns doing the head versions, and monitoring their partners. Whenever the child doing the head versions loses eye contact with his partner, the partner calls this to his attention. As in using the mirror, it is critical that this eye contact be maintained. Again, the balance board may be employed when the child has become adept.

keys to improvement   1   The child performs all three head versions with ease, and without body movement, while maintaining proper eye fixation.

2   The child successfully carries out these activities while maintaining balance on the balance board.

Figure 1. (Cont'd.)

monocular rotations

purpose To develop smooth automatic rotations of each eye and to help develop the child's ability to separate centering (what he is thinking about) and alignment (what he is looking at).

equipment 1 Ball and string. Ball can be up to 3" in diameter. Insert a long eye screw through the ball and secure with a washer and nut. Attach the string (nylon fishing line works well) to the eye of the screw.

2 Eye cover. An eye patch can easily be made by cutting out an oval piece of cardboard and attaching it to a rubber band or piece of string.

set up

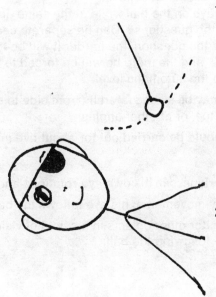

1 Hang the ball from the ceiling so that it will be about twelve inches above the child's chest as he lies on his back, directly beneath it. By inserting the other end of the string through an eye screw in the ceiling and another eye screw on a nearby wall, the ball becomes adjustable for height. The string can be pulled and wrapped around a cleat on the wall, raising the ball when not in use.

2 Place the patch over the child's left eye.

procedure 1 The child lies on the floor with the ball suspended over the center of his chest. The child should be relaxed, with his feet slightly apart, his arms slightly out from his sides and his head straight. You or a helper should observe that his two sides are mirror images of each other.

2 The ball is moved so that it makes a circular motion, swinging slowly in a wide arc at first. Later the circumference of the circle and the speed of the ball may be varied.

3 With his left eye covered, the child follows the ball with his right eye, twenty times clockwise and twenty times counterclockwise. The eye patch is then placed over his right eye and, using his left eye, he again follows the ball for twenty rotations in each direction. The child should follow the ball accurately, keeping his eye on the ball at all times, without jerky movements. He should be closely observed either by yourself or a helper, and reminded **every time** his eye loses contact with the ball.

Figure 2. **Source:** See [3]. Reprinted with permission.

4   As the child finds it easier to keep his eye on the ball, he should be encouraged to become aware of other things in his field of view. For example, as he follows the ball, you or a helper might hold up fingers and ask him how many you are holding up. Or, you might ask him to point to other things in his visual field. He should become reasonably adept in simply **following the ball** before additional demands are placed upon him.

5   As the child's proficiency increases further, you or the helper should begin asking him questions as he follows the ball. These might relate to school assignments, or they could involve counting numbers backward, addition of numbers, or similar questions.
Can the child keep his eye on the ball while at the same time thinking about, and answering, the questions? Can he separate centering and alignment? The harder the question, the harder it will be for him to keep his eye on the ball, and the more he will be forced to drive his visual tracking down to the automatic level.

6   For variation, the ball may be swung laterally from side to side, or vertically from head to toe, or at other angles.

7   **Monocular rotations** should be carried out for about five minutes per training session.

keys to improvement

1   The child recognizes jerkiness in his own eye rotations and movements.

2   There are no more jerky movements; his eye follows the ball smoothly.

3   The child is able to monitor other objects in his field of vision and answer questions while following the ball.

Figure 2. (Cont'd.)

sensory-system matching

purpose To develop in the child a speech-auditory, kinesthetic (motor) and visual match regarding fixations and direction.

equipment Set of four sensory matching guide sheets, supplied with program. A metronome may be employed if available, but it is not essential to the procedure.

set up

Attach guide sheet 1 to a wall in a well lighted room at about the child's eye level. It should be located so that the children can stand approximately five feet in front of it. (As an alternative you may wish to make transparencies from the guide sheets. By projecting on a screen, or on the wall, it is possible to work with an entire class at once if the children are of approximately equal ability.)

procedure 1 Have each child stand in front of the guide sheet and move his eyes in a rhythmic manner from left to right, and down the sheet, as if he were reading. He will call out "oink" or "quack" as he fixates upon the pigs and ducks. The child should strive for an **even cadence,** regardless of how slowly he must go to achieve it.

(A primary purpose of step 1 is to gain an idea of each child's ability to apply an internal rhythm to the challenge, fixate, and maintain cadence. The children should then be arranged into approximately equal groups of five or six, the number that can comfortably work with a guide sheet at one time.)

Figure 3. **Source:** See [3]. Reprinted with permission.

2   Replace guide sheet 1 with guide sheet 2. Working in small groups the children will call out the direction of each arrow rhythmically; up, down, right or left. The individual children should strive to match the external rhythm of the group.

(As the children work with the more difficult guide sheets, you may wish to change your groupings, depending upon each child's ability to function effectively with his group.)

3   The children will look at guide sheet 2 and move both hands, palms outward, in the direction of each arrow. They should continue to strive for smoothness and rhythm in their responses.

4   Steps 2 and 3 are combined. The children respond to the arrows both kinesthetically and verbally. The pace should be as fast as the children can go, **so long as they maintain an even cadence.**

5   Use guide sheet 3. The challenges of guide sheets 1 and 2 are now intermixed. The children will respond to the sound of the animals, and to the direction of the arrows. The verbal response to the animals is combined with a verbal **and** kinesthetic response to the arrows.

6   Use guide sheet 4, which intermixes blank spaces with the objects of regard. The children respond as in step 5, but make neither a verbal nor a kinesthetic response when their eyes come to a space. For purposes of cadence, however, they treat the space as if it contained an object; the next object of regard should be called at the same instant it would have been called if the space **had** contained an object.

7   When a group is able to handle this challenge rhythmically, you should increase the pace by clapping your hands, or setting a beat on a metronome. You may also increase the challenge by coding their response. For example, have them use the left hand to point left, the right hand to point right, lift the left foot when saying "oink", the right foot when saying "quack", and do nothing during a space.

keys to improvement

1   The child is able to match his internal rhythm to an external rhythm.

2   The child is able to match motor activities with internal and external rhythm.

3   The child is able to match speech activities with internal and external rhythm.

Figure 3. (Cont'd.)

Figure 3. (Cont'd.)

Guide Sheet 1

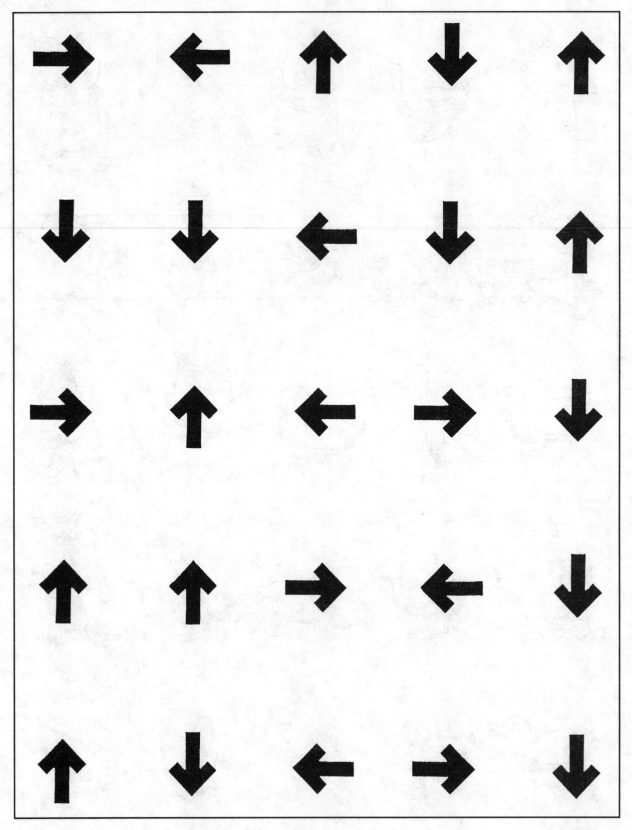

Figure 4. **Source:** See [3]. Reprinted with permission.

Guide Sheet 2

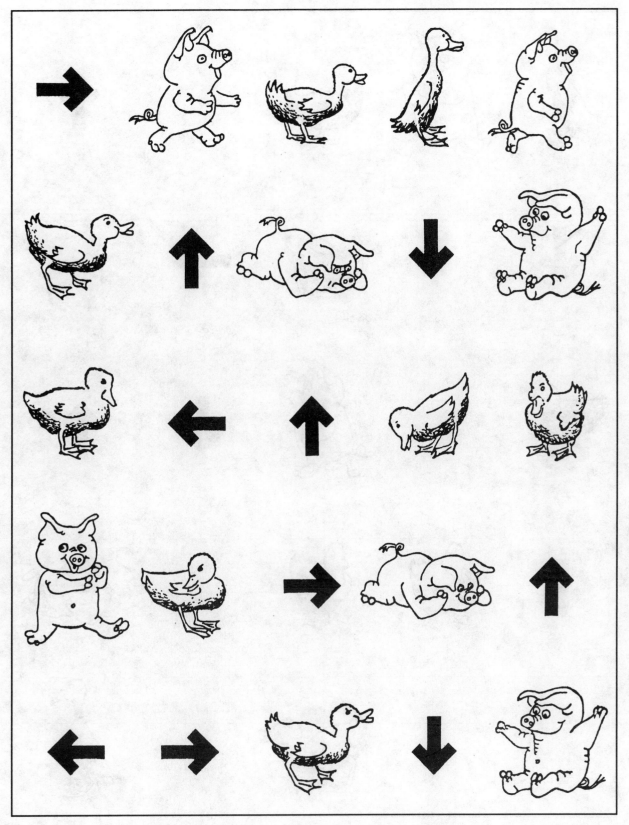

Figure 5. **Source:** See [3]. Reprinted with permission.

Figure 6. **Source:** See [3]. Reprinted with permission.

Guide Sheet 4

We cannot leave this chapter without at least mentioning the child who was not ready for kindergarten, but who was enrolled anyway, because his birthday fell before a certain date. At the Pre-K Screening, he may have behaved more like a three- or four-year-old than a five. His parents were adamant when the subject was raised, and suggestion offered that perhaps he needed another year at nursery school or even just a year at home to grow and become more independent and confident. So he came to school, not very happy about it, and has struggled all year. He is now not ready for first grade, despite all our efforts to help him. There are some things that time alone can help. Now the question looms: What to do? There are several choices. Probably the easiest for all except the parents would be to let the child continue (not "stay back") in kindergarten. Another choice, if the school district provides one is a pre-first grade, or "developmental" first, as it is sometimes called. Still one more alternative that would be acceptable for the child and some parents is: transfer to a private kindergarten in the area for a year, and then back into the public school for first grade. The only choice *not* to be considered is promotion to grade one. Having seen it happen, with sad consequences for the child and ultimately, for the parents as well, we have become advocates of *Is Your Child in the Wrong Grade?* [4]. We have several copies of it along with *Don't Push Your Preschooler* [5] in our school library for parents' use.

One of the most important thrusts of the Child Development Program at John Adams School in North Brunswick, New Jersey, has been its preventive aspect—preventing learning disabilities, preventing school phobia, and preventing kindergarten failures. It takes considerable effort, but is extremely gratifying. What takes a lot more effort is trying to remediate learning disabilities that are allowed to continue untreated for years. Then we have to deal with the negative attitudes and feelings of poor self-worth that layer themselves on top of the original problems which might have been something as easy to correct as not being able to copy accurately from the chalkboard.

REFERENCES

1. G. N. Getman, E. R. Kane, M. R. Halgren, and G. W. McKee, *Developing Learning Readiness*, McGraw-Hill, New York, 1968.
2. A. J. Kirshner, *Training That Makes Sense*, Academic Therapy Publications, San Rafael, California, 1972.
3. A. C. Heinsen, *Visual Motor Development*, Learning Opportunities, San Jose, California, 1973.
4. L. B. Ames, *Is Your Child In the Wrong Grade?* Modern Learning Press, Rosemont, New Jersey, 1978.
5. L. B. Ames and J. A. Chase, *Don't Push Your Preschooler*, Harper & Row, New York, 1974.

CHAPTER 3

How the Child Development Program
Helps in First Grade

At John Adams School in North Brunswick, New Jersey, many of the kindergarteners who are promoted to grade one are reading. They have learned to blend sounds together to form words and have also learned that some words don't look the way we expect them to by "sounding them out." Thus, we have put to use the visual-memory skills we've been developing in kindergarten to learn words such as "the," "was," "of," "look," etc. commonly referred to as "sight" words. At the same time, we have laid the foundation for phonics, letting the youngsters know that usually a word is produced by blending together the sounds of its letters from left to right. This, after all, provides the motivation to learn the letter names and sounds.

All this comes easily to some and with great effort to others. Some of these first graders are newcomers to North Brunswick, and may never have experienced anything like our developmentally stimulating kindergarten. Those who are struggling with the sounds and symbols as they enter grade one find solace and an opportunity to review the basics presented in a slightly different way with the Child Development Program. Perhaps four or five in each first-grade classroom need this extra review, reteaching, and reinforcement. We try to set them into the schedule for Child Development sessions immediately following their classroom reading lesson. One of the first things we use is the *Clymer-Barrett Prereading Battery*[1] which assesses the children's abilities to recognize letters, find words that match, identify pictures of things that begin with the same sound, and others that end with the same sound, supply missing lines to complete a design, and copy a seven-word sentence. The results obtained serve as a guide to help us map out our strategy in working with these students. At the end of each child's participation in the Program, the alternate form of the test is given and we can measure the progress that has taken place very specifically.

Because it is so important as a foundation for reading and language arts, we usually begin with a review of the names and sounds of the letters. We use a variety of techniques which combine visual, auditory, kinesthetic, and tactual input to help the children learn these as quickly as possible. As soon as they have mastered a few consonants and vowels, we start to blend them into words. One of the favorite helping tools is the object box, a key feature of the *Intersensory Reading Method.*[2] In it we find a tiny plastic apple, bottle, comb, dog, egg, etc. As we explain to the children that we are using only the beginning sound of each item, we can set the little comb down on a piece of blank paper, getting them to isolate the first sound,

---

[1] *See* Appendix.

[2] Intersensory Reading Method: Originally obtained from Book-Lab, Inc., has been out-of-print for a number of years. The object box can be assembled fairly easily using small items which begin with all the sounds, including th, ch, sh, and wh.

"c." Then we set the little apple down, and after eliciting the "a" sound, we show them how to blend these two. As we set the little table next to the comb and apple, the more perceptive ones in the group will offer to finish the word "cat." Then we can demonstrate how simple it is to make a new word by just changing the first sound: by removing the comb and replacing it with a tiny feather, or a little horse, or a pen.

When we have worked with a variety of beginning sounds, we can move on to ending sounds, using the same technique. The middle letter, always a vowel, of course, is changed only after they have a solid handle on the beginning and ending sounds. By now, the children are usually ready to substitute small letter cards for the objects. We start putting words into brief sentences, and those who may have been non-readers in September are sailing along in the *Primary Phonics*[3] book series within a month or two. We also review the vocabulary of the storybook that is being used in their first grade reading group. Some of the words will be phonetically regular, and others will be "sight" words. Now we can help them to recognize the difference. While they are still at the first stages, it is important, we feel, to set up the conditions for success. We want to keep their interest without over-challenging them. When a word is phonetically regular, we can encourage them to "sound it out" for themselves. When it is a "sight" word, we explain that this is one they must look at as they listen to the teacher say it and then try to remember it every time they see it again. We use the same technique of initial letter substitution to help the children become more familiar with their vocabulary words.

In recent years, with some schools adopting the "whole language" approach to reading, we are finding the need for Child Development Program input more important than ever with regard to the "at-risk" children. Now, more than ever before, the students who are unsure of the sound-symbol relationship of letters are slipping through the cracks as they sit with the whole class, hearing the story read by the teacher from the "Big Books." If they should memorize the story as they hear their classmates repeat it, they might lead the teacher to believe that they, too, know how to read. What a rude awakening comes when they need to read something new on their own. As we are now being told by some fifth- and sixth-grade teachers, "Some of these children cannot read!"

It has been our experience that when we perform a motor act, it tends to leave a more lasting impression. The Child Development teacher helps the first graders in the Reading Review and Reinforcement Program by demonstrating the correct formation of each letter while practicing printing and focusing skills, both of which are crucial to accurate replication. By using *Zaner-Bloser*[4] color-cued paper which has a dark blue line, then light blue line, then red line, and actually verbalizing the correct formation of each letter as we produce it, we guide the child as if holding his hand while walking through still unfamiliar terrain. For example, while printing the letter "b" on the chalkboard, which we have previously prepared with the same three colored lines, we would say, "Starting on the dark blue line, we go straight down all the way to the red, forming the bat, then bounce up to the light blue line and circle to the right, forming the ball. Now we have our bat and ball which form the letter 'b'." It's easy to remember the difference between "b" and "d" after this lesson as we point out that when the letter begins with the bat, it's a "b", but when the "dish" comes first, it's a "d."

[3] *See* Sources.

[4] *See* Sources.

The word "bat" begins with a "b" and "b" begins with a "bat." "Dish" begins with a "d" and "d" begins with a "dish."

We practice printing the vocabulary words for which the children are responsible in their classroom, and make rhyming words for each. Then we print words that mean the same, and words that mean the opposite. We use anagram letters to form words, and make a game of it that the children enjoy: "How many words of three or more letters can you make in three minutes?" This can be followed by four or more letters in four minutes, etc.

We create our own stories so the children will realize that what we read is simply "talk that's been printed on paper." As the group dictates a story, the Child Development teacher prints it on either the chalkboard or large poster paper while each child copies it on lined paper. We pace ourselves appropriately, i.e., if we are at the very beginning level of this activity, we may do one letter at a time. We proceed gradually to one word at a time, and then one sentence at a time. We ask the children to watch while we print, and then we watch them while they print, which gives us the opportunity to check on their formation of the letters and placement of them on the page. When we've finished the printing, we illustrate the stories and mount them on the bulletin boards in the corridor. Children take great pride in their work when it is given such prominent display. The entire school population walks past our door daily, as do all visitors to the building.

To vary our activities, we sometimes read stories into a tape recorder, then follow the words with our eyes as we play the tape back. If the children have made any errors, they may discover them on their own, or a neighbor will offer the correction.

After six weeks or so of these activities, some of the youngsters have caught up and polished their skills well enough to move up to a more advanced reading group. The children who need to continue in the Child Development Program seem happy enough as we do more challenging activities, such as unscrambling sentences about "City Mouse and Country Mouse," printing them and reading them. They are proud to take these home to read to their parents, and are aware that reading is becoming easier for them.

We use some of the eye movement exercises from the kindergarten Child Development Program because, usually, these first graders were not in our school the year before. We use the Heinsen exercises ("oink, quack, up, down," etc.) and the near-far visual fixation exercises along with the chalkboard circles for peripheral awareness from *Developing Learning Readiness*. We also use the *Controlled Reader*[5] to help them develop speed and accuracy in reading. As an exercise in visual discrimination, each child is asked to view three letters for one second, and tell which one was different. As the filmstrip continues to move to the next row of three letters, the next child must be ready to look, see, and decide which one is different. If they can't work that fast, we set the timing mechanism to accommodate, so that they can be successful. Once they've achieved the correct response, our goal will be to do the same activity a little faster. Then we can go to four letters per line, or three words per line. The children enjoy this procedure. It stimulates them to be successful at something they know is helping them to read better and faster, while at the same time it's a challenging game.

---

[5] Controlled Reader: now called Guided Reader may be in your school's inventory already. If not, it is now available only for use with computers. *See* Sources.

As we move along, the first graders still in Child Development are also getting practice in re-reading the stories from their classroom readers. We discuss them, to be certain the children are comprehending what they have read. We talk about what happened first, next, and last. We practice changing sentences into questions, and review proper capitalization and punctuation. We have fun matching the endings of sentences with the correct beginnings. We use *Sight Word Lab*[6] to extend the children's sight vocabulary. There really is no end to the variety of activities we can do with first graders who need review and reinforcement in reading and language arts.

While more children at this grade level have difficulty with reading and writing, some find math troubling. Although our elementary grades are now supplied with buckets of small wooden blocks of different shapes and colors to encourage the children to manipulate, create patterns, and develop an awareness of basic mathematical understanding, some still don't grasp it. The classroom teachers will refer these to the Child Development teacher for review and reteaching, a different way. We can start with counting games that require motoric involvement, such as a variation of "Giant Steps." Using a large mat of plastic about 6' by 9' scored into rectangles, we line the children across one end. Then we might say, "Billy, take three steps forward and one to the right." Billy must repeat the directions prefaced by "May I . . . ?" before he moves. If he forgets to ask, Billy loses his turn, so this game also teaches concentration on rules and procedures, as well as directionality. As Billy walks, he counts aloud, and the numbers take on new meaning. The object of the game is to be the first one across the mat. We count things around us and things at home: how many chairs are there at your kitchen table? How many people live in your house? How many cans are there in your pantry? After we have explored our surroundings to discover how many of this or that there are, we proceed to putting things together and taking them apart. Still in the here and now, we stand Jenny and Carol at the front of our group, and review "One girl plus one girl equals two girls." When Jenny is sent to her seat, how many girls are left? If this sounds much too easy, it might be. But if we want these children to understand math, we have to start at the beginning and build from there.

We continue to experiment and gradually progress to the level of using flannel-board figures of trees or flowers or frogs, telling little stories while the children manipulate the figures to match what is happening in the tales they are hearing. After they are comfortable with the verbal and representational, we move on to *Structural Arithmetic*[7]. This is a wonderfully organized, tangible way of teaching math to the slow learner. With wooden rods of varied colors in lengths from one to ten inches, notched to enable the user to feel how many each rod represents, the children are encouraged to compare and experiment. Each child can discover that when the purple rod and the white rod are laid end to end, they are the same length as the yellow rod. With the use of the white subtraction shield, we can cover up part of the yellow rod and discover that the remainder is the same length as the purple rod. Given the opportunity to experiment in this manner under the guidance of the Child Development teacher, many children who have been "in the dark" about math have had the light turned on and their confidence restored. *Structural Arithmetic* has three levels, corresponding roughly to grades K-l, 2, and 3. Each has a workbook and a teacher's manual.

[6] *See* Sources.

[7] *See* Sources.

While the Child Development teacher and the classroom teachers have been conferring regularly but informally, progress reports on each child are prepared every marking period, keeping the parents and administration informed. We also have two regularly scheduled conference sessions with parents (one in November, the other in April) and are available for others when requested.

In first grade, the most obvious problems in learning arise in the reading/ language arts and math areas. We have found that early intervention has been very successful in eliminating or relieving these difficulties. Occasionally we find a child who is not progressing enough to move on with the group. We discuss our concerns with the classroom teacher and principal. By March, we usually can tell who is still having trouble, and after discussions with the parents, we have two options: first, if we suspect a deeper problem, we request that the Child Study Team evaluate the student and bring their report and recommendations back to us. The second option, if the student in question is very young for the grade, or very immature, might be to continue at this grade level. Through educating parents about the value of such a placement, we have saved many children from a school career doomed to struggles and frustration. The parents who have followed our suggestions have come back years later to thank us for helping their children to become successful and confident students.

CHAPTER 4

The Remedial Aspect

As Dr. Jay Roth, the school psychologist who originally saw the need for this Program, stated:

The Child Development Program emerged as a carefully developed response to a serious challenge.

The challenge was clear. Many children who had the ability to perform were simply not functioning at the level of their ability. A study of these children revealed that a majority of them, especially in the primary grades, were unable to perform due to what is generally termed perceptual and/or motor difficulties. These children often then developed attitudes about their own inability to perform tasks as efficiently as their peers and this attitude was invariably negative and destructive. They began to see themselves as failures and this vision was constantly reenforced in the classroom. Furthermore, the classroom teacher knew little or nothing about such disorders, and even if she did, she would need both time and materials to deal with them. Many of these children were of average or above average ability yet were failing and since perceptual difficulties often affected general intellectual functioning as measured by evaluation, then it was often felt by teachers that many of these children were "slow" which they were not.

What was needed was the meeting of four conditions:

1. Teachers were going to have to learn what these problems were about and how to deal with them;

2. Some method for having these children in small groups had to be devised without having them placed in special classes with all that implies;

3. Special nonacademic techniques had to be directly presented to the child in a coherent and orderly fashion so as to have his progress systematically evaluated; and

4. It was of primary significance that the teacher, who was presenting these techniques, establish a warm one-to-one relationship which could be therapeutic in the sense that the child could feel accepted as worthy and valuable, regardless of his functioning. This would enable the child to operate on what he has rather than on the negative picture he had of himself.

Dr. Roth continued:

It is felt that all these conditions were met by the introduction of the Child Development Teacher, an experienced teacher specially trained during in-service programs and specific course work, (who) would work in individual schools under the principal of that school, and be part of the school assuming all non-academic duties. Both formally and informally the CD teacher would then take referrals from teachers and after careful evaluation, establish small groups meeting with them daily so that an intensive and ongoing relationship could be established. The presentation of specific techniques within the atmosphere of an accepting and warm relationship was and is the key to the success of this program.

The Child Development Program is based on the premise that all children require the development of perceptual-motor integration at a level consistent with their motivational state and their chronological age in order to maximize their abstract, cognitive, and social development.

A second premise is that learning is related to one's own feelings about one's self, and therefore, that which can affect one's sense of worth and achievement directly affects learning itself.

Based on the above premise, a program has been devised in the general area of perceptual and motor development which is persistent and ongoing so that those children selected and involved are receiving continual, positive reinforcement in the form of recognition, attention, and warmth. These reinforcements, built around those areas weakest within the children involved, directly affect the child's functioning and sense of worth regarding that functioning [1, pp. 1-2].

Although these words were written twenty-seven years ago, they are as timely as if they had been written yesterday. North Brunswick, New Jersey, has been meeting the challenge all these years, helping children with learning difficulties to overcome their failure, confusion, negative self-image, and fear of school.

The Child Development teachers have been working with children who exhibit any or all of the following:
  1. Lack of general and specific coordination
     a Eye-hand
     b. Right-left, etc.
  2. Inability to see relationships between self and environment
  3. Inability to develop good relationships between self and others
  4. Sensory problems such as: auditory, visual, tactile, kinesthetic
  5. Problems dealing with recall:
     a. Auditory memory
     b. Visual memory
     c. Motor memory [1, p. 2]

To put it another way, Dr. Roth had observed that some young children were having problems learning because they had difficulty gathering and/or processing the information being presented by their teachers. For a variety of reasons, these children had trouble with the very basic intake systems: they appeared to listen but as soon as the teacher finished giving directions would ask, "What should I do?" The other children would begin their assignments, but these few would require step-by-step repetition of each item to be done.

These were also the children whose gaze would wander from the point at which they had been directed. It was not unusual for these youngsters to start off "paying attention" to the line of print on the chalkboard only to be distracted a minute later by the bright ribbon in the hair of the child sitting in front of them. Needless to say, when the teacher called for a volunteer to supply the missing word or letter or number, the child who was looking at Susie's hair bow had no idea what the teacher was talking about.

These children also had trouble producing, i.e., printing, cutting, drawing, pasting, folding, etc. because their coordination was inadequately developed. Not only was it a problem to hold a pencil correctly, but to get the point of the pencil to hit the proper line on the paper and form the letters the way the teacher had demonstrated was almost too much to demand. Then to have to remember to leave a space in certain places: What did they want from him, thought this hapless child. It was all he could do just to get himself into the correct seat without tripping on his shoelaces (which never seemed to stay tied), or knocking something off the desk next to his. Why were his crayons always on the floor? Why could he never find what he was looking for in his desk? How come his papers were always torn by the time he was on the third line? Why was it so hard for him to learn to cut and paste neatly like the other kids? He was trying as hard as he could. Maybe he was just dumb he thought.

Their inability to succeed in the classroom was robbing these children of their self-esteem and causing some of them to react to their frustration with antisocial behavior. Joey would give up trying to cut out those pumpkins and cats, ending up with piles of orange and black scraps of paper on his desk, his lap, and the floor. He would glance at Katie's perfect productions and try to sneak them over to his desk. When she demanded he return them, he'd crunch them up in his fist as he gave them to her. Maybe, as he explained to the teacher, he hadn't meant to mess them up, but the frustration was building, his feelings of self-worth plummeting.

Other children with these difficulties might react with such passive and quiet behavior as to become almost invisible in the classroom. These were the students who seemed to get by trying to duplicate whatever the child next to them did. Sally never knew what was going on in the classroom. She just tried to put the same squiggles on the same part of her paper as David did because the teacher was always patting David on the head and saying, "Good work!" When called on to respond to a question, these children who would never volunteer, would simply sit, mute. Eventually, the teacher would call on one of the others who were waving their hands vigorously, anxious to give the correct answer, and silent Sally would feel even worse about herself.

The original concept of the Child Development Program was to change the child through the various techniques described in the following chapters and thereby help him to become more successful in his classroom.

More specifically, in Roth's words:

The Child Development Teacher was presented with the following objectives:
1. The development and integration of the sensory and motor areas in order to allow the child successes in the classroom that would be otherwise unattainable because of his or her developmental difficulties.
   a. The development and awareness of large muscle activity
   b. The ability to transfer and generalize self-concepts and body locations
   c. The psychological integration of fine and gross motor activities

    d. The ability to move one's body in an integrated way

    e. The development of directional orientation

    f. The development of tactile discrimination

    g. The establishment of homolateral hand, eye, and foot dominance

    h. The development of primary auditory, visual, and motor skills

    i. The ability to receive differential auditory stimuli

    j. The development of auditory sequencing

    k. The development of differential visual acuity

    1. The ability to visually differentiate the forms and symbols in one's environment

    m. The improvement of visual memory

    n. The development of visual-motor fine muscle coordination

    o. The ability to learn visual-motor spatial form manipulation

    p. The ability to express oneself in language

2. The development of social skills involved in problem solving.
    a. The ability to get along with one's peers
    b. The ability to anticipate the consequences of a social situation by inference
    c. The development of the feeling that the child is valuable
    d. The development of the feeling that school can be a place which is personal, warm, concerned, and accepting

3. The development of the curriculum to better meet the needs of individual children and to better meet specific problem areas.

4. To assist parents and teachers, acquainting them with the etiology and significance of the numerous developmental and perceptual difficulties encountered by children; and also demonstrating and assisting in new methods of educational remediation. Also, to act as a resource person for the school, the administration, the staff, and the parents in the general area of individualized instruction and learning problems.

Guidelines for selection of children included

1. Referral by classroom teachers for various reasons such as:
    a. Performing below grade level
    b. Poor attention span
    c. Doesn't complete assignments
    d. Hyperactivity/hypoactivity
    e. Difficulty with visual and auditory symbols
2. Referral by Learning Disability Specialist or School Psychologist as a result of psychological testing.
3. Referral by Principals when they are aware of the necessity and sometimes following a parent/principal conference.
4. Observation by Child Development Teacher during classroom visitation [1, p. 3].

    The Child Development Program is designed to recognize and ameliorate the child's specific learning problems. Because such a child may have different levels of ability in various areas of performance, a series of tests are administered to reveal his strengths and weaknesses in the following categories:

1. Auditory Perception
   a. Screening by school nurse for hearing deficiency
   b. Discrimination of initial, medial, and final sounds
   c. Identification of common sounds
   d. Memory and ability to follow oral directions
2. Visual Perception
   a. Screening by school nurse with telebinocular for visual acuity
   b. Discrimination of likenesses and differences
   c. Constancy of shape: discrimination of shapes and sizes
   d. Position in space: discrimination of reversals and rotations of figures
   e. Spatial relationships: analysis of simple forms and patterns
   f. Figure-ground: ability to perceive figures against increasingly complex backgrounds
   g. Visual-motor: Gesell copy form and completion test
                    Bender Gestalt
3. Gross Motor Coordination
   a. Hopping
   b. Jumping
   c. Skipping
   d. Walking
   e. Balancing
   f. Catching
   g. Throwing
4. Fine Motor Coordination
   a. Cutting
   b. Connecting dots
   c. Printing and/or writing
5. Body Awareness/Directionality
   a. Recognition of body parts
   b. Differentiation of left and right [1, p. 4].

By establishing a teacher in each elementary school who would work with these students and help them develop the skills they needed for learning, the Child Development Program became the answer to many parents', teachers', and children's prayers. We took all those children who needed help and led them through some of the same exercises in coordination, balance, form perception, etc. that we now use for all of our kindergarten students. They never had these opportunities presented to them before, and were ready to do anything to escape their classrooms where probable failure loomed.

For some of these children who were called "hyperactive" because they could not stop squirming in their seats, the release of pent-up energy afforded just by walking from their classroom to the Child Development room was therapeutic. But the real boost came from learning how to control their movements. When they performed each of the exercises outlined in the *Teachers' Manual* of *Developing Learning Readiness* three times successfully on three consecutive days, they could move on to the next level. We supplemented these coordination exercises with the eye-movement activities as described in *Visual Motor Development* [2]. Gradually, the children learned how to control their movements, how to get their hands and eyes to work together. The chalkboard activities helped them to develop their peripheral vision so they could take in more information at a glance. To strengthen the little muscles in their fingers, we had exercises using pinch clothespins and coffee cans. We pulled on strong elastic bands and squeezed rubber balls. Added to these were desk level activities such as games of sequential organization, *Ann Arbor Tracking*[1] books for better eye movements, and thinking games to develop auditory memory.

Some of these activities could be done simultaneously, i.e., combining a motor development exercise such as bouncing and catching a playground ball with an auditory memory game like "I went to the market and bought apples." The next person in the group was to bounce and catch saying, "I went to the market and bought apples and bananas," and so on. This combination kept the attention focused on both the motor and the auditory memory: a little more challenging, and a lot more fun.

In 1968-69, the first year of the Child Development Program in John Adams School mornings and Maple Meade School afternoons, we worked with more than fifty children in small groups throughout the year. All of these were referred by the teachers, psychologist, or learning consultant. The reasons for referral ranged from "lack of motor coordination" to "lack of emotional control." Many of these children were potential candidates for Special Services evaluation, which was a lengthy process involving a visit with the school social worker, an examination by the school psychologist, an educational evaluation by the learning consultant, plus numerous conferences with the teacher, principal, and parents. Meanwhile, usually, the non-performing or underachieving child who was the subject of concern, might languish in the classroom for months, waiting. (The law now demands action on these referrals within 60 days of receipt.)

The introduction of the Child Development teacher into North Brunswick Schools produced *immediate* intervention in these children's lives. Often the very day that a referral was handed in by the classroom teacher, the Child Development teacher would start the process of inclusion. By setting up an appointment to observe the child at work, his problems were analyzed in terms of functioning in the classroom. Some had more deeply-seated difficulties than others, as was discovered through the individual testing which followed, usually within a week. Conferences with the teachers and parents followed to keep them informed. Each child was assigned time in the Child Development schedule, for the exercises and activities appropriate to remediate the conditions which had been described by their teachers. As they learned to do various things that they could not do before, they began to feel better about themselves, and were more willing to try other techniques which were presented to them. Within the small group in each Child Development session, a feeling of acceptance and friendship developed. The children soon learned that they were there to improve their skills, and they must never laugh at each other's expense. They were taught never to say, "I can't!" but always to say "I'll try!" A feeling of support and encouragement developed, and most of the children grew more successful.

Inevitably, some progressed more rapidly than others and were released from the Child Development Program as they developed the skills needed for classroom success. As some left the groups, others were enrolled. Several still needed to be evaluated by Special Services and ultimately were placed in special education classes, but most progressed satisfactorily and moved along in the mainstream of education, feeling good about themselves. Each one

[1] *See* Sources.

was better off for having been involved in it, and each participant had pleasant memories because of it.

Recognizing the enormous impact the Child Development Program could make on a child's life, I was absolutely hooked. Having had experience as a second- and then a first-grade teacher, I had been aware of the gratification felt when a child in my class left knowing more than when first starting that grade. But for these special children, learning was much more difficult. When I thought about what might have happened to many of them had the Child Development Program not been there, I realized that this was probably the most significant contribution I could make in my lifetime. Writing about it to help others get started in doing the same lifesaving activities was something I always intended to do. That's why I saved all of my log books and some of the more interesting case files.

The material is as appropriate today as it was years ago. Here's hoping more schools will start using the Child Development Program to help children become more successful.

REFERENCES

1. J. Roth, *Report to North Brunswick Board of Education,* pp. 1-5, March 21, 1969.
2. *Visual Motor Development,* Figures 3, 4, and 5 (see Chapter 2).

CHAPTER 5

Meaningful Interventions

Many years ago, when we were taking education courses to become certified as teachers of K-8, we were taught how to teach children to read, use crayons creatively, and master the operations of arithmetic. In not one course do we recall being taught the importance of proper posture at the desk, proper pencil and scissor grips, proper lighting, and sound nutritional practices. Not even at the master's level were we given insight into the tremendous changes that can occur in a child's performance when proper and meaningful interventions are introduced and are monitored regularly.

Having been educated to the importance of each of the above as a result of attending many lectures and seminars by and for developmental specialists including psychologists, optometrists, neurologists, nutritionists, and occupational therapists, we have tried to share our awareness with teachers, administrators, parents, and most important of all, the children. Amazing improvements can take place through the implementation of fairly simple and basic changes.

PROPER POSTURE AT THE DESK

According to Dr. Darell Boyd Harmon, engineer and physiologist, the optimal distance from eyes to near work is the distance from the elbow to the first knuckle [1]. The top of the desk should reach the bottom of the chest. Some desks are adjustable for height. The school custodian can make the necessary changes in a few minutes. If your school is equipped with desks that can be set to slant at a twenty-degree angle, consider your students fortunate. In his research, Harmon found this to be the optimal surface for reading and writing. If your desktops are flat and not adjustable, simply screw two metal doorstops to the upper back corners of a 12″ × 18″ piece of plywood. Attach two rubber knobs to the lower back corners to prevent the plywood from slipping off. A narrow lip of quarter-round moulding at the bottom edge keeps books and papers from sliding off (see illustration). The student's chair should be low enough to permit both feet to remain on the floor, with the buttocks pressing into the back of the seat. Leaning forward slightly, the weight is placed on the thighs and hips. Both arms rest on the desk, holding the book or the paper and pencil. This is the posture to be encouraged for all reading and writing tasks.

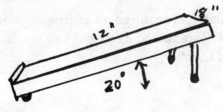

DON'T permit children to read or write while lying down on the floor or in bed. Unnecessary stress is being placed on the eyes when in those positions.

DON'T permit the child to lean down over the desk, bringing eyes close to the paper. Remember the "Harmon distance," which usually measures 12 to 14 inches.

DON'T permit the child to cradle his head down on one arm while reading or writing. This causes a distortion of the body and can also block the vision from one eye partially or completely. If the child complains that this is the only way he can see the material he is writing, it may be due to improper pencil grip.

Use of the non-writing hand and arm is important as it supports the upper body, keeping it in balance. Placed across the top of the paper, which slants from bottom left to top right for the right-handed person, the left arm and hand also anchors the paper to the desk so that the writing hand can move freely across the page. It should be noted here that the position of the paper for the lefthanded writer is angled in the opposite direction, i.e., from top left to bottom right, the non-writing hand and arm resting across the top of the page [2].

The peripheral vision which we worked to develop at the kindergarten level is as important in the writing process as it is in reading. When you can see the whole 180 degrees in front of you, the central task flows more evenly and you can sustain the effort for longer periods of time with less fatigue.

DO permit frequent breaks in visual attention. Encourage children to look up across the room from their near work for a few seconds every ten or fifteen minutes. This will increase, not diminish, capacity for work, as well as decrease eye strain. Getting up and stretching every half-hour or so is also good for relieving tension and stimulating circulation in the body.

PROPER PENCIL GRIP

Holding the pencil loosely between the thumb and pointer, resting it against the knuckle closest to the tip of the middle finger, at least one inch from the pencil point is what the experts define as the proper pencil grip. It produces the least amount of stress on the fingers, wrist, arm, shoulder, and neck while permitting both eyes to view the tip of the pencil, guiding it through the writing process. This description applies for both right- and left-handed people. If the fingers are placed too close to the tip of the pencil, the writer must lean forward and to one side to monitor the writing, producing a stressful posture and distortion of vision.

Once an improper pencil grip has been established, it is very difficult to change. It's best to encourage the correct grip from the beginning (pre-school), but if it's too late for that, there are several devices on the market to help overcome this problem:[1] small triangular plastic pieces that fit over the pencil, they are available from school supply companies as well as most stationery stores.

Unfortunately, if Mom or Dad has acquired an improper pencil grip, Junior is almost sure to imitate it, so be on the alert. Parenthood carries many responsibilities, and demonstrating the proper pencil grip is one of them.

---

[1] *See* Pencil Grippers in Sources.

PROPER SCISSOR GRIP

Insert the thumb in the top hole, the middle finger in the bottom hole, with the pointer finger cradling the bottom of the center. This stabilizes the scissors so that by merely lifting and lowering the thumb, the cutting can be directed smoothly forward. Special scissors are available for left-handed children and should be provided so that they can maintain consistent hand dominance. There are also scissors available now that cut well with either hand doing the job. Cutting, like writing, requires the use of both hands to work well: one for holding and turning the paper, the other for directing the scissors.

PROPER LIGHTING

If your school is not yet equipped with full-spectrum lighting, this should be at the top of the shopping list. Full-spectrum fluorescent lighting is the next best thing to natural light, according to photographer/researcher John Ott. This lighting is credited with reducing hyperactivity in children and encouraging higher productivity in the classroom under calmer conditions [3]. Proper lighting at home includes overhead lighting from 150 to 200 watts, with supplementary lighting from desk or floor lamps. Avoid high-intensity lamps; too much light is as hard on the eyes as too little.

PROPER NUTRITION

No one will argue with the statement that growing children need the basic food groups and regular meals, including a nourishing breakfast. Sometimes we hear of a child who has "no appetite" in the morning. This child must be encouraged to eat at least a slice of toast and a glass of juice or milk before leaving for school. He can take along a healthy snack such as fruit or a small muffin to eat mid-morning when the appetite finally awakens. Since most of the child's work is done in the morning, it is vital that the body be supplied with vitamins and minerals which provide the energy for proper functioning.

It has been reported that sugar causes hyperactivity in some children. Years ago, the first choice of remediation for students with short attention span was a sugar-free diet. This required careful monitoring, time-consuming shopping trips (reading labels on everything edible) and children who were mature enough to decline a treat offered to them at a birthday party or during school lunch time.

We had PTA meetings featuring nutritionists as speakers and sent information to parents in our school newsletter. We even published recipes for "healthy" muffins made without sugar for those interested. Our traditional PTA fundraising bake sales were changed to pretzel sales, and John Adams School definitely had a calmer and cooler climate.

The use of Ritalin, a drug to curb hyperactivity has been successful with some children if used carefully and minimally. While not advocating its use, we are merely reporting that it has brought about desired results in a number of children: a diminishing of hyperactivity and an increase in the student's ability to concentrate, take in information, follow directions, and produce satisfactory written work in an acceptable time frame. The various side effects of Ritalin have been documented and the final choice is made by the parents after conferring with the pediatrician in all cases.

NO-ROLL CRAYONS[2]

Just because they stay where they are placed, these crayons deserve wider recognition. They also make interesting designs when used creatively, since they have one flat side and one curved side.

PROPER GRADE PLACEMENT

At the beginning of each school year, we screen new arrivals to North Brunswick. For K- and first-graders, the Child Development teacher uses the BRIGANCE® K-1 Screen (both levels are included in one testing manual, with different answer-sheet pads for each grade.) For second- through sixth-graders, the Reading Specialist screens for reading level, and the Child Development teacher checks math skills, using the *Steenburgen*[3] for grades two, three, and four. For grades five and six, we use the math book end-of-year tests from grades four and five respectively. The screenings give us a really clear picture of which skills need reteaching if these newcomers are to be programmed for success.

Occasionally, a child will appear with no records from the sending school. His parent will tell us the grade level, yet after the reading and math screenings, it seems the child is far below his expected level of achievement. True, it doesn't happen every day, but we did have this experience several times and here is the best way we discovered for dealing with it. First, confer with the principal, showing the results of the screenings. Then, confer with the parent and the principal, offering interim placement pending receipt of the child's school records. The interim placement should be the grade where the child will be most apt to fit into the academic skill level, based on the screenings just completed. Offer to move the child up to the next grade if his work demonstrates that he is clearly beyond the interim placement within the next two-week period (which is about the time required to receive his records from the sending school district). For various reasons, some parents cannot accept having their child remain in the same grade for two years. They move to a different school district, expecting to be able to place their child where *they* think he belongs. For the best interests of all involved, we assert our right to determine the correct placement. There are enough problems awaiting a child when he moves into a new school without adding the extra burden of being a couple of years behind in academic skills. When the records arrive, we sometimes find that the child was being referred for a Special Services evaluation, or that the previous teacher had recommended another year in the same grade. Either situation requires additional testing of the child, but at least we have already placed him in a situation which is not completely unrealistic while we move along to identify and remediate his problem.

IMMEDIATE MATH CLINIC

The Math Clinic, conducted by the Child Development teacher usually starts the day after the screening is completed. Beginning with all the new sixth graders in one group, if space and time schedules permit, we meet for about twenty minutes daily, going over the test together on the chalkboard, since it is supposed to be review material at that point. If anyone

[2] *See* Crayons in Sources.

[3] *See* Sources.

had trouble with a specific item or method of solving it, we do it again step-by-step. We do not return the tests, so the students' attention is focused on the chalkboard. Then we try several similar examples on the board. We don't move on with the review if anyone has a puzzled look on his face. The rest of the test is reexamined as a group effort in the same manner.

The exception to this procedure occurs when a student is obviously "lost." This is the one who has completely forgotten fractions, for example, or who claims, "We never had that in my school last year!" It's quite possible, especially in today's highly transient society, for a child to have been in several different schools during a year. The chapter on fractions might have been lost in the shuffle. Rather than subject all the others to a complete and redundant reteaching at this point, we will progress through the remainder of the test. After the rest of the group is dismissed from the Program, the one student who needs it will come back for however long it takes to learn about fractions and whatever else he might have missed.

We use the same procedure for students in grades five and four who need to fill in some gaps in their math foundations.

For the most part, the children who attend the Math Clinics do not have learning difficulties. They were just unfortunate to have missed some presentations for whatever reason. Once these lessons have been taught, the students are dismissed from the Child Development Program, assured by the knowledge that they now can do whatever it was they had trouble doing on the screening test.

IMMEDIATE HANDWRITING CLINIC

The time slot vacated with the completion of the Math Clinic is then available for our Handwriting Clinic, open to students in grades four, five, and six who have not learned cursive writing yet, or whose writing is so slow, unsure, labored, or illegible as to be a deterrent to their success in their classrooms. The Handwriting Clinic is usually conducted a minimum of three times weekly, for about fifteen minutes each session.

In the many years that we've been doing this, we have tried quite a few different techniques. Our very favorite is an adaptation of the *Johnson Handwriting Method*,[4] using special paper called "Cursive Writing Forms" (see Sample "A"). Johnson follows a format of grouping letters that begin with the same stroke, not alphabetically. I have found the use of the Cursive Writing Forms supporting the verbal, visual, and motor example which I demonstrate on the chalkboard to be successful consistently.

We do four letters per page this way: I request that the students watch my chalk (green, yellow, orange, or purple, large soft chalks work best). I have previously prepared the chalkboard by drawing three horizontal lines: dark blue, light blue, and red in descending order, with a line maker. The lines are about three inches apart. Then I have made many white lines intersecting the horizontal lines at an angle that corresponds with the angle on the Cursive Writing Forms. The colored lines match the handwriting paper used in our Child Development Program from grades three through six. The lines simply get closer together as the grade level climbs. This paper is available from *Zaner-Bloser*[5] as well as many school supply firms.

[4] *See* Sources.
[5] *See* Sources.

Sample A.

After I demonstrate the first letter on the chalkboard, simultaneously verbalizing the process, I hand out copies of page 1 (see Sample "B"). Then I watch while the children trace the first letter on their cursive writing forms. At first, I repeat my words for them. As they repeat their tracing five times, they are encouraged to say the words with me while they continue across the page. I move among the desks (there are rarely more than 6 or 7 at one time), checking to see that each is starting in the correct spot, using the slanted lines properly, and keeping up with the group. As we develop the skill, we can increase the speed.

This is what it sounds like while we do the first four letters:

(i) "First you watch mine and then I'll watch yours. Start in the bottom left corner of the first box. Curve up to the middle right, slide down the line, anchor it at the baseline, curve up to the middle again, release and dot. Now, again, curve up, slide down, curve up and dot." I repeat the words in a rhythmical way, urging them to follow suit, "Curve up, slide down, curve up and dot." Again, I check to make certain that all are using the slanted lines on the paper, sliding their pencils down, then up, and releasing them from their papers at the middle line.

When they have completed the first line of i's, we go through the same steps for the (u), with the colored chalk on the board. This time we say, "Curve up, slide down, curve up, slide down, curve up, release."

Three major control strokes are emphasized in the *Johnson Handwriting Method:* the down stroke, anchored to the baseline, the swing up (or curve up) and the release. Dr. Johnson explained that if these three strokes were consistently and correctly produced, the writing would always look neat. The ingenious Cursive Writing Forms make it very easy to be precise. If they follow the rules, success is assured, even with students who have been diagnosed "neurologically impaired." When working with children who have severe motor difficulties, I have altered the procedure to include several preliminary sessions using finger paints to encourage smoother strokes. Shaving cream on a formica desk produces a similar slippery surface to develop the smooth curves we need in cursive writing. The next step for these special needs children was tracing and copying large size letters on the chalkboard, followed by a cursive writing form with much more space between the lines, as shown in Sample "C."

We continue with the next "curve up" letter, (w), for which the script is "Curve up, slide down, curve up, slide down, curve up, bridge, release." The release always takes place on the middle line. If there is another letter to hook on to, it's ready. If it's the last letter in the word, that's fine. All the other words end on that middle line as well, and the writing looks very neat.

The final letter on Sample B, page 1 is (t) which is done with, "Curve *way* up the line, slide way down the line, anchor to the baseline, curve up to the middle, release and cross" (see Figure 1 for instructions of other letters).

The same four letters which appear on the bottom half of the page are taken home for practice and brought back to the next session. Once the children have mastered the correct formation and placement of the letters, we make the transition to their blue-and-red-lined paper. If they still need the Cursive Writing Forms for words, we have it available (see Sample D), but we don't want them to become dependent on those slanted lines once they can do without them.

The lower-case letters are completed first, and the children are encouraged to start using them in their regular classwork immediately. Within a week to ten days, an improvement in

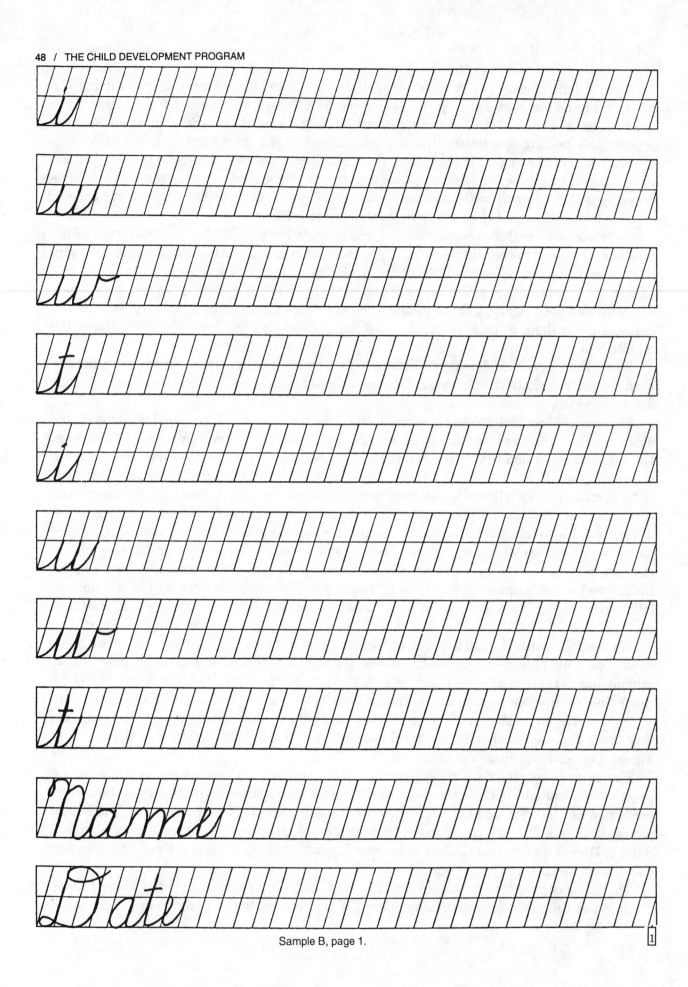

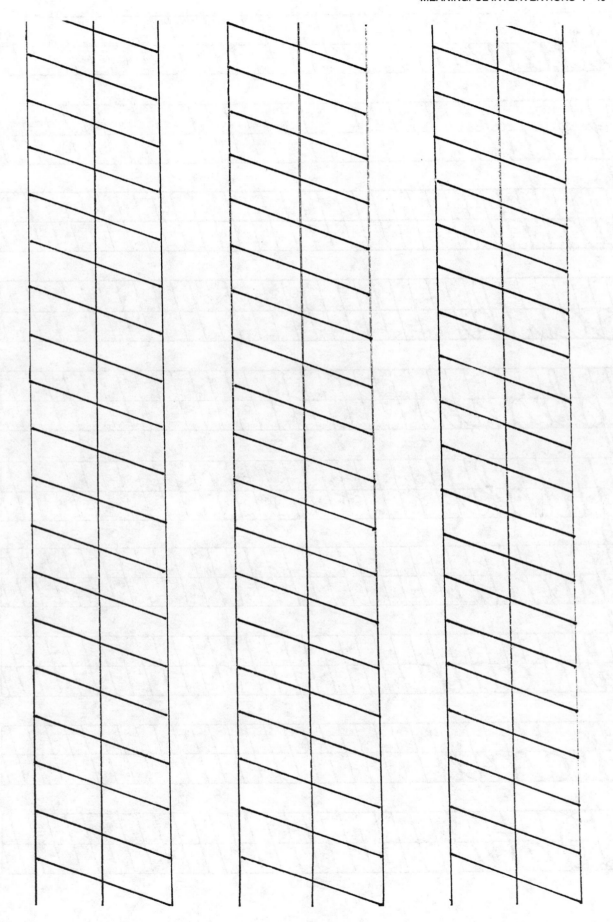

Sample C.

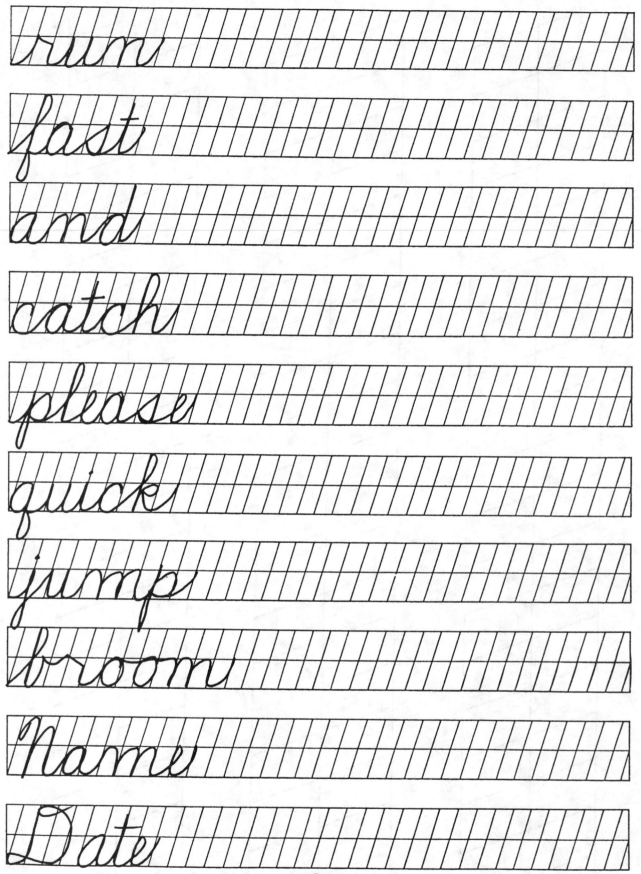

run

fast

and

catch

please

quick

jump

broom

Name

Date

Sample D.

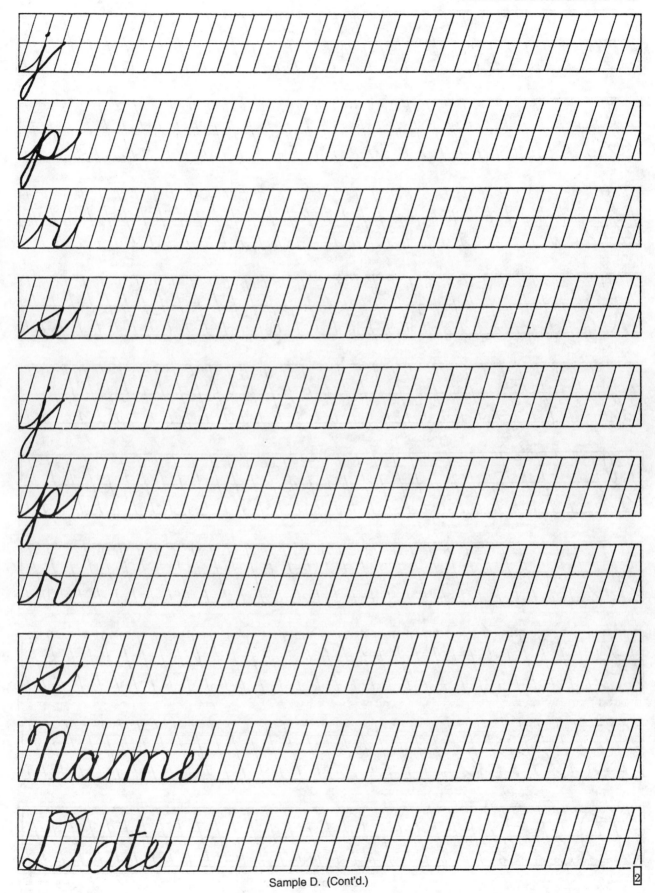

Sample D. (Cont'd.)

e

l

h

k

e

l

h

k

Name

Date

Sample D. (Cont'd.)

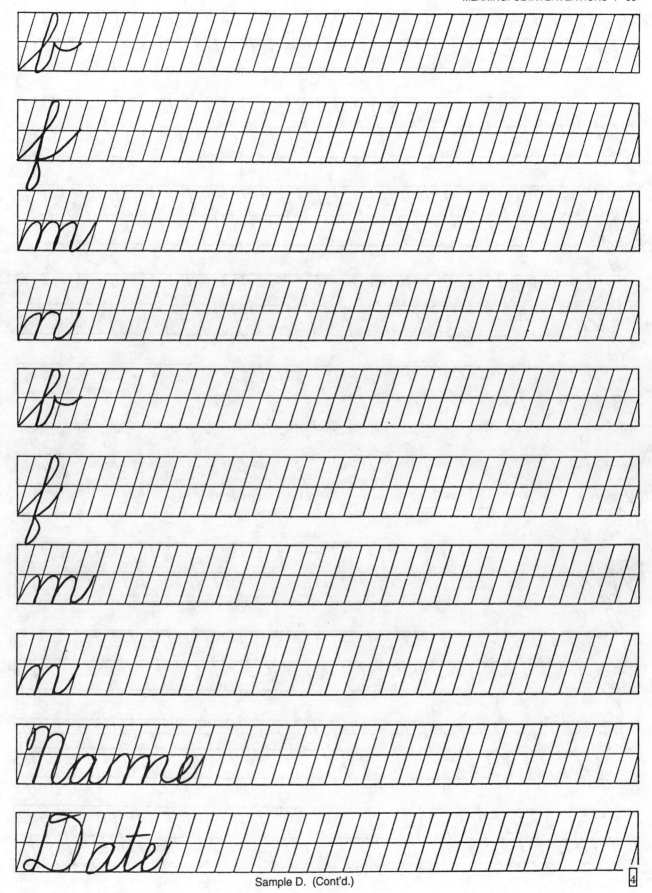

b

f

m

n

b

f

m

n

Name

Date

Sample D. (Cont'd.)

w

x

y

z

w

x

y

z

Name

Date

Sample D. (Cont'd.)

5

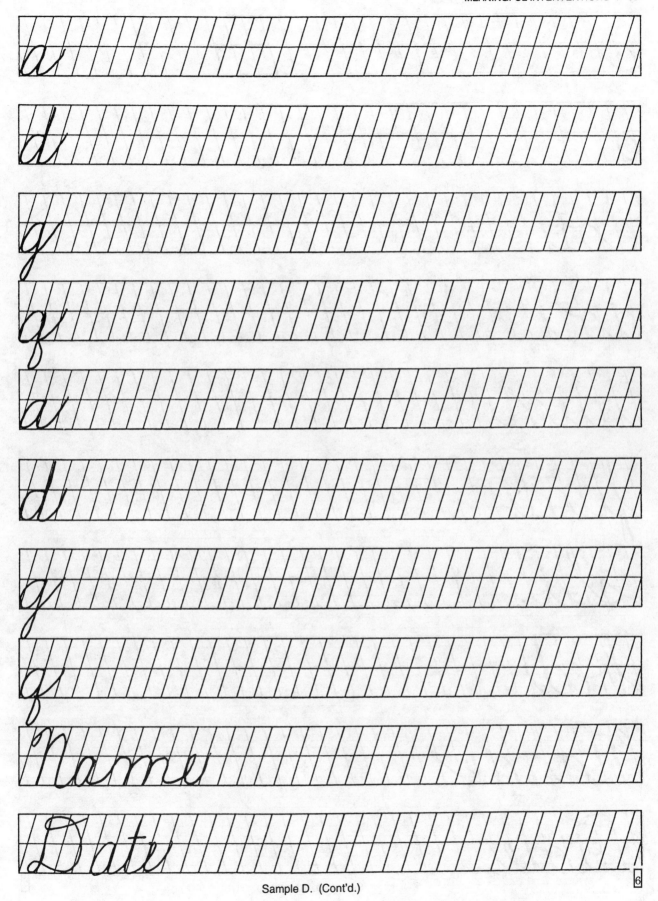

Sample D. (Cont'd.)

c

a

cot

dot

run

fun

sled

bed

Name

Date

Sample D. (Cont'd.)

7

Sample D. (Cont'd.)

Sample D. (Cont'd.)

Sample D. (Cont'd.)

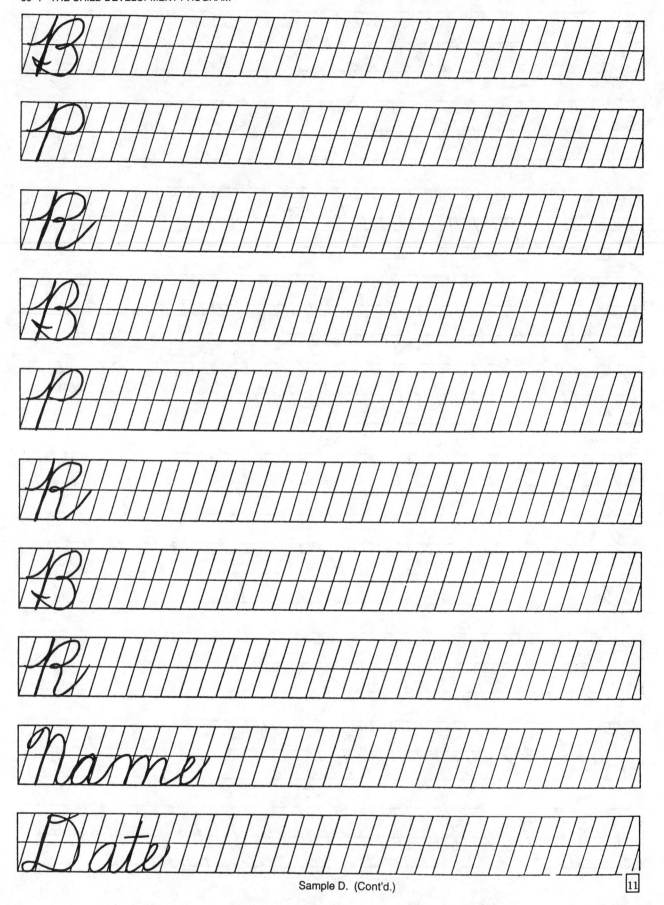

Sample D. (Cont'd.)

11

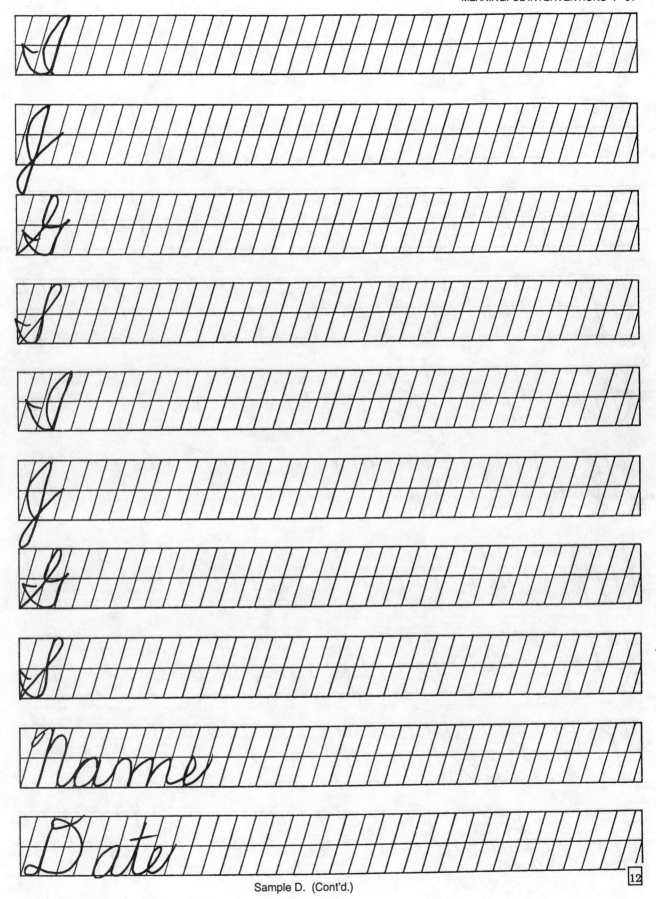

Sample D. (Cont'd.)

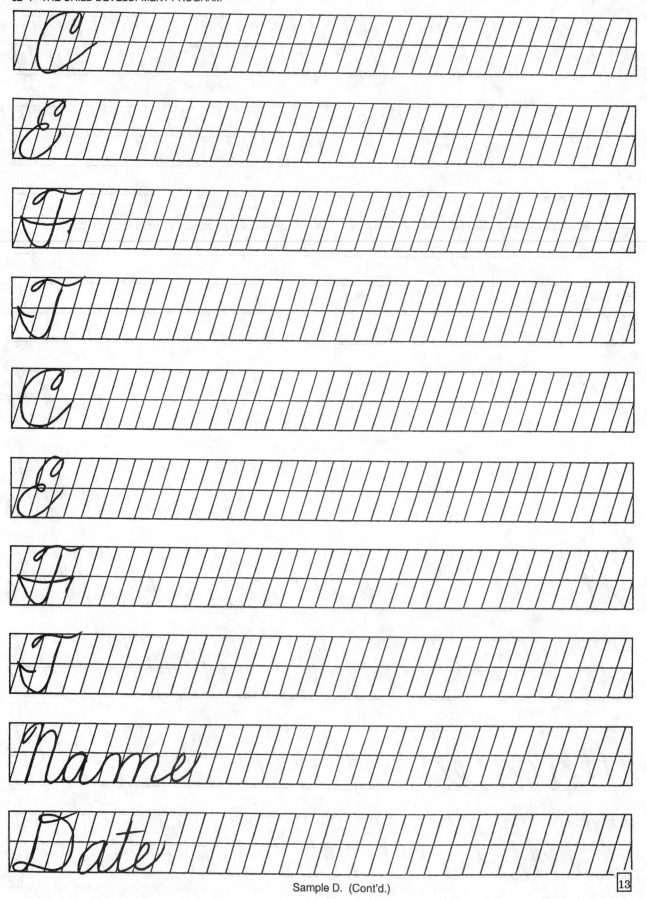

Sample D. (Cont'd.)

13

Sample D. (Cont'd.)

their handwriting is apparent. Then we start the capital letters. Samples of each page in the series, along with the scripts which have been so useful, and some practice papers with which the children have enjoyed working are included (see Sample "E"). They are asked to trace the first word on the top line, then copy the same word on the line below, continuing in this manner across the page and finish it for homework. At the next session, we can always tell which children followed these directions. The papers that are neat and evenly spaced belong to the ones who have traced and copied one word at a time, building their motor memories and practicing their skills. Those who trace the whole line of words first and then try to copy the whole line invariably run out of space before they've completed the sentence. These students will get a new page to do, with double lines separating the words, to remind them to trace one, copy one, trace the next, copy the next, and fit their words directly under the words I've written on the page. When the words are framed in this manner, it's really hard to go wrong.

In transferring their best handwriting to their classwork, the children are urged to improve in one subject at a time. Usually, their spelling words become our practice words, so it's easy for them to excel both in spelling and handwriting on their weekly tests. From there, I suggest that they include book reports and any other papers that they know are going to be displayed on the bulletin boards in or near their classrooms. Finally, social studies assignments and letters to their grandparents are targets for "neat writing" awards.

Rarely will a child need more than a month or six weeks, at three sessions per week, to develop clear, neat handwriting. If the motivation is there, it can happen faster. One of our fourth grade teachers always held good handwriting in high esteem. She would not allow her students to use ink until they had met her standards in pencil. This became a major incentive and we witnessed some really remarkable improvements in even less than one month.

While we have been conducting the Math and Handwriting Clinics primarily for newcomers to the school, there are sometimes a few of our previously enrolled students with learning difficulties who can and do benefit by being included in the review of both subjects. Depending on the individuals and their needs, we schedule them in the regular clinics, augmenting this reteaching with extra motor development exercises or spatial awareness sessions. We might use "taffy pulling" with very large, strong rubber bands, and clothespin pinching to develop the tiny muscles in the fingers and hands. We roll and pinch chunks of clay and use the long strips of it to form letters. We also weave potholders to develop the children's manual dexterity as well as their eye-hand coordination.

On the chalkboard, we use some of the exercises from *Developing Learning Readiness* as a starting point and then continue with elaborations such as the following which further develop peripheral awareness and eye-hand coordination. While looking at the central X, the child uses chalks in both hands simultaneously to form lines that start on a chalkboard-drawn pattern resembling a clock face. With right hand on the "6" and left hand on the "12," lines are drawn toward the X and back to the number, repeating this without stopping ten times. The next set of lines is made, still looking at the X, with right hand on the "5" and left hand on the "11," going in and out, toward the X and back to the numbers without stopping ten times. The remaining sets of lines are formed in a similar manner, moving each hand to

Name

1. Irene and Sam live in Illinois.

1.

2. Jack and Jill jumped for joy.

2.

3. Tyrone and Teresa tasted the turnips.

3.

4. John Adams is a good school.

4.

Sample E.

Name:

Date:

1. Patty and Peter pet the pony.

2. Ruth and Robert ride the rocket.

3. Ben and Barbara bake blueberry pie.

4. Alice and Andy ate all afternoon.

Sample E. (Cont'd.)

Name:

1. Gloria and Grant got groceries.

1.

2. Susan and Sam sold stamps.

2.

3. Lilly and Luke love lollipops.

3

4. Dinah and Donald dig diligently.

4

Name

1. Carol and Curtis can copy clearly.

2. Ella and Evan eat eggs at Easter.

3. Oliver and Oscar operate on others.

4. Uncle Umberto is under the umbrella.

Sample E. (Cont'd.)

Name

1. We love the month of December.

1.

2. We have holiday parties, and

2.

3. get toys and have fun.

3.

4. We are thankful for all we receive.

4.

Sample E. (Cont'd.)

We have completed a review of the correct formation and placement of all cursive letters.

We promise to write legibly.

Sample E. (Cont'd.)

Scripts for Cursive Letters

These are to be used aloud while first forming the letters on the chalkboard (see page 45 of Chapter 5—Handwriting Clinic). Starting point for most lower case letters is the bottom left corner of a box on the Cursive Writing Form. The release point for all lower case letters is the middle line. i, u, w, and t are included in the text.

j: Curve up to middle right, slide down the line through the baseline, swing up to the left, then over to the right, crossing at the baseline. Release and dot.

p: Curve up, slide down, swing up to the left, cross the baseline, circle around to the right, then swing up and release.

r: Curve up just beyond middle right, slide down to the middle and cross over to the next line. Slide down, anchor to the baseline, swing up to middle right and release.

s: Slant up, slide down and anchor to the baseline, swing left, swing right, and release.

e: Curve up, loop over to the left, slide down and anchor to the baseline, curve up and release.

l: Curve all the way up, crossing through the middle of the slant line. Loop over to the left, slide down the line, anchor, curve up and release.

h: Curve all the way up, slide all the way down, then bounce back up the slant line with an overcurve, touching the middle line and continue down the next line, anchor, curve up and release.

k: Start as if making the h. Right after the overcurve, curl in to form a small loop, then swing down and right to the baseline, curve up and release.

b: Start as if making the l. At the base of your downstroke, curve up close to the loop, touching the middle line, bridge and release.

f: Start as if making the l. Continue the downstroke to the top of the next set of lines, loop up toward the right, swinging closed at the baseline, then curve up and release.

m: Curve over, slide down the line, anchor. Curve over, slide down the line, anchor. Curve over, slide down the line, anchor, curve up and release.

n: Same directions as for m, but one less "Curve over . . ."

v: Curve over, slide down the line, anchor, curve up, touch the middle line, bridge and release.

x: Curve over, slide down the line, anchor, curve up, release and cross from baseline up.

y: Curve over, slide down the line, anchor, curve up, slide way down to the top of the next set of lines. Loop up to the left, cross at the baseline, and release.

z: Curve over, slide down, anchor, loop down, swing up to the left, cross over the baseline and release.

The next six letters have a different starting point: just below middle right.

a: Curve left, close the oval, slide down the line, anchor, curve up and release.

d: Curve left, close the oval, keep on going up to the top and then slide down, anchor to the baseline, curve up and release.

g: Curve left, close the oval, slide down all the way, loop up to the left, crossing at the baseline and release.

q: Curve left, close the oval, slide down all the way, loop up to the *right,* closing at the baseline, curve up and release.

c: Curve left, touch the baseline, curve up and release.

o: Curve left, close the oval, bridge and release.

Figure 1.

The first eleven capital letters start with the clockwise oval loop near a top left corner on the Cursive Writing Form. Once that loop is mastered, the rest of the letter flows easily. Remember, you are using the script *while demonstrating the letters on the chalkboard.* The children can say it with you as they trace the first letter on the line of their paper. Give them time to trace at least three times and practice across the line. Then go on to the next letter.

H: Down, up to the left and over, slide down the line. Leave a space, and lift up to the top, slide down the line, anchor, bounce up toward the first line, curve under and out to release.

K: Down, up to the left and over, slide down the line. Leave a space, and lift up to the top, slant down to the middle, curve over, then down, up and release.

M: Down, up to the left and over, slide down the line to the baseline, bounce up the line almost to the top, curve over, slide down the next line, bounce up not quite as high, curve over, slide down, anchor, curve up and release.

N: Start as for M, but one less "curve over."

W: Same beginning strokes. From bottom of first line, slant up to top of next line, slide down, anchor, curve up and over to release at the top.

X: Start with the loop, then curve down to the left, release at the baseline. Leave a space. Start at the top, curving counterclockwise, ending in a loop at the bottom right. Be sure both lines touch in the middle.

U: Start with the loop, slide down the line, anchor, then curve up to the top, slide down the next line, anchor, curve up and release in the middle.

V: Start as for U, but as you curve up to the top of the second line, swing over as on the ending of the W and release.

Y: Start as for U. On the second slide down, keep going through the baseline, to the top of the line below, loop up to the left, cross at the baseline, curve over and release.

Z: Start with the first half of the X, then a tiny clockwise loop on the baseline, curving into a long loop below, swing up and release on the middle line.

Q: Start as for Z; right after the baseline loop, dip into a bridge below the baseline and release.

A: Start in top right corner, curve left, close oval, slide down the line, anchor.

O: Start in top right corner, curve left, close oval, loop under and release at top line.

B: Start on middle line, with an undercurve to the top, slide down the line, anchor, bounce up the same line, curving to the right at the top, tuck in with a tiny loop on the middle line, then out again, round the bottom, swing up to the line and back to the right. Release.

P: Start as for B, but pull in and close up the curve on the middle line. Release.

R: Start as for B; as you tuck in on the middle line, curve over, then down, up and release on the middle line.

Figure 1. (Cont'd.)

I: Start at the baseline, curving up clockwise to the top of the same line; slide down, anchor, swing up to the left, touch the middle line, swing down to the right and release.

J: Start as for I, continuing the down stroke to the top of the line below, swing up to the left, curve to the right, cross at the baseline, release at middle.

G: Start at the bottom left corner, curve up, crossing at the middle line and continue to top, swing over to left, slide down to the middle line, forming the loop; swing across forming a bridge into the next upper right box, then slide down the line to the baseline, curve up to the left, crossing the beginning stroke, swing back and release.

S: Start as for the G. After you have formed the top loop, slide down the line, curving up to the left, then swing back to the right and release.

C: Start at top right with a short slant down, swing up to the right, curve to the left, touch the baseline, curve up and release.

E: Start as for C; tuck in with a tiny loop on the middle line, curve toward the left, touch the baseline, curve up and release.

F: Start near the top of a line, slide down, touching the baseline as you curve up to the left, touch the middle line, swing a bridge across three spaces to the right, then slide down the line and release above the baseline. Return to the top box above the beginning of the bridge, make a loop with a wavy tail that covers all three spaces.

T: Start as for the F, but stop just as you begin to swing the bridge across the three spaces. Return to the top and make exactly the same wavy tailed top stroke.

D: Start at the top of a line, slide down, swing to the left on the baseline, making a small oval as you cross the downstroke and continue across the baseline, two spaces, curve up to the left, close up the top and cap it with a bridge, release at the top.

L: Start on the middle line with an undercurve up and across two spaces. Curve up and over the top to the left, slide down the line to the baseline, anchor, swing to the left, forming a small oval as you cross the downstroke, with a bridge that dips below the baseline, then swings up to it and release.

As the children become more familiar with the letters after lots of practice, all of these strokes become routine, and don't need the precise language as given. It will help them to review the script if they run into trouble with a particular formation.

Figure 1. (Cont'd.)

the next number on the clock, until all numbers have been used. There are other variations of this exercise, such as calling out two numbers between 1 and 12: "Left 10, right 2." The student must follow the directive without moving his eyes from the X. The main thing to remind the student is, "Keep your eyes on the X at all times, but be aware of your hands and the lines they are making. Count as you work, and try to develop a smooth rhythm, making the same lines over and over."

Many more suggestions for developing visual-motor skills can be found in the next chapter.

When a child is completing the work in his classroom with confidence and care, the teacher will let us know. We see each other daily in the faculty room, in the office, at meetings, and in the halls. We prepare written reports in November, February, April, and June with one copy for the parents, and one for the teacher, which the principal reads first. We all keep in touch, and when we feel that the child is able to work independently, even if this requires a temporary modification in the length of his assignments, we will present him with his "Certificate of Achievement" from the Child Development Program, with a firm handshake or hug, and a very proud smile. We always let him know that the door remains open. If he feels he needs help with anything in the future, he knows it's okay to come and get it. Just knowing that sometimes makes the shaky ones a little more confident. Looking at the work each has done from the beginning of his participation in the Program to his departure is always cause for celebration. Each one knows he's improved. Each takes his folder of work samples with him, to show the teachers, friends, and family. The growth in self-esteem is not measured in numbers, but in posture and facial expressions: the straighter back, the set of the shoulders, the head held high, the positive look in the eyes, the confident smile that says, "I can do it!"

Probably 90 percent of the children in the Child Development Program each year leave under these circumstances. Those who do not are the ones we must refer for evaluation by the Special Services Child Study team or confer about with parents, teacher, and principal with an eye toward giving the child more time at this grade level. It is rarely used, but is sometimes the best alternative for a very young child. As a voice of experience, I will admit that it doesn't always work. If a parent is against it, it won't work. But for those who have no apparent learning disability, and just need a little more time, it's the best thing we can give them. Parents have come back to thank me for suggesting it when they see how happy, confident, and successful their children become the second year in the same grade.

There are always exceptions, of course. A few children each year have made progress but not enough to be truly independent and successful. These are the youngsters we plan to continue in the Child Development Program in September. Sometimes we find that they have heeded our suggestions of various activities which can be practiced during the summer and are quite self-sufficient in the fall. In every case, we meet with the next teacher to determine whether the child would benefit from continuing in the Child Development Program. We try never to abandon a child who is still in need of help.

REFERENCES

1. D. B. Harmon, *Dynamic Theory of Vision,* self-published, Austin, Texas, 1958.
2. N. S. Cohen, O.D. and J. L. Shapiro, O.D., *Out of Sight Into Vision,* Simon and Schuster, New York, pp. 132-137, 1977.
3. J. Ott, based on research done with the Environmental Health & Light Research Institute, as reported by Jacob Liberman in *Light: Medicine of the Future,* Bear & Company, Sante Fe, New Mexico, p. 58, 1991.

CHAPTER 6

Developing Visual and Motor Skills

One of the most valuable features of the Child Development Program is the flexibility built into it. It gives the Child Development teacher considerable freedom in using a variety of methods to help the child to develop skills he has not yet mastered. Thus, the Child Development teachers in North Brunswick have had the opportunity to use whichever techniques worked best for them in helping youngsters to learn. At the beginning, we met weekly for two hours to discuss our current cases and the techniques which were bringing the most success. Through this sharing of information, we developed our own awareness of the wide variety of training activities at our disposal.

While there have been books published listing suggestions for educating children with various learning problems, many simply give strategies to cope with the problems. For example, if a child had difficulty with paper-and-pencil activities, the solution was to put a computer at his disposal. If a youngster had trouble copying from the board, the strategy offered was to give him a task that required him merely to underline the correct answer in a workbook.

Our attitude in the Child Development Program is: Don't just change the requirements; change the child. Lead him, one step at a time, through the various exercises that will develop his ability to do the task he was unable to do before. His personal accomplishment of the tasks that he has observed others in his class doing is the key to his heightened self-esteem. With this in mind, we are now ready to share some of the methods we've used to bring about amazing changes in children.

"Readiness for learning" is discussed in detail in the introduction to *Developing Learning Readiness*. It is neither appropriate nor necessary at this point to expound on theories governing human growth and development. Getman and his associates state the child develops and learns along a hierarchy starting with *movement* (creeping and crawling), continuing through *orientation* (Where am I? Where is it?), to *identification* (What is it?), and *communication* (How does it work? Tell me/show me more about this). Most significant is the need for the individual to experience these for himself. His parents and teachers can only set up the conditions for these stages of learning to evolve. We cannot do it *for* him, but we can provide the opportunities for this learning to occur.

Learning takes place through movement. We start with large motor activities and then refine skills through the use of smaller muscles. Here are some of the tried and proven favorites:

1. The first three Programs of *Developing Learning Readiness*:
   (a) Practice in General Coordination (starting with Head Roll while looking at specific targets)

(b) Practice in Balance (walking beam while maintaining visual fixation on targets, developing peripheral awareness along with coordination and balance)

Variations include practice in walking, jumping, hopping, and skipping down a hallway, while fixating on a distant central target. Prior to the lesson, tape large red X's on walls and as student sets out, have him look at the central target while simultaneously counting the red X's aloud as he passes them.

For those who have not yet learned to skip, we have a very structured step-by-step method of teaching them:

A. Set up *Stepping Stones*[1] (flat rubber squares approximately 7″ x 7″ x 1/4″ with numerals 1-10 printed on top) with #1, 3, 5, 7, and 9 on the right for right-footed[2] children (left for left-footed), and the #2, 4, 6, 8, and 10 on the other side (see Illustrations 1 and 2).

B. Ask the child to walk it through, matching the name of the foot with the number of the stepping stone, i.e., "Right-one, left-two, etc."

C. Next, remove the #2 stone.

D. Child is to hop on right foot from #1 to #3, then put left foot on #4, and walk out the rest of the steps as described in B.

E. Remove #5 stone.

F. Child is now to hop on right foot from #1 to #3, then hop on left foot from #4 to #6, stepping with right foot on #7, left on #8, right foot on #9 and left on #10.

G. Repeat this procedure of alternate hopping a few times, then rearrange stepping stones to look like this: (see Illustration 3).

H. Child is now encouraged to hop on right foot from #1 to #2, left from #3 to #4, right from #5 to #6, left from #7 to #8, and right from #9 to #10. This produces what we call "slow motion skipping."

I. Repeat enough times to develop the motor memory and then move out to the hallway or playground black-top to practice the newly developed skill of skipping without the stepping stones. Sometimes a musical background helps to provide the accelerated rhythm desired. We have the stepping stones painted in white on our macadam play area near the kindergarten in both configurations, as shown in Illustrations 1 and 3, as well as a hop-scotch set-up and large circles for other games.

(c) Eye-Hand Coordination (specific exercises at chalkboard).

Follow directions for above in *Teacher's Manual* of *Developing Learning Readiness* (pages 53 through 65).

2. *Visual Motor Development,* awareness level creeping starting with hand-knee movements on floor. Follow directions on Figures 1a, 1b, and 1c.

3. Rocking board approximately twenty-four inches square with non-skid surface, mounted on a 4″ x 4″ x 2″ block is used to develop left-right awareness. To rhythm,

---

[1] *Stepping Stones,* your kindergarten may already have a set of these. The manufacturer has discontinued the numerals and is now producing only letters on the Stepping Stones. The reverse side of each is blank, so you can put the numerals on with permanent felt-tip marker, or adapt the directions in the illustrations to use letters instead. The order number in Sources is for the *capital* letters.

[2] *Right-footed:* to determine which foot a child favors, ask him to kick a ball several times, or ask him to print his name on the floor with his toe.

Illustration 1 (right-footed).

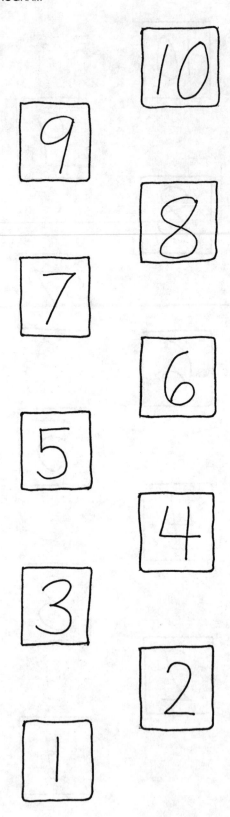

Illustration 2 (left-footed).

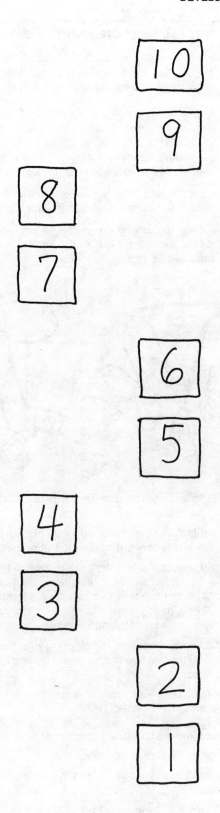

Illustration 3 (right-footed).

awareness level creeping: bilateral

purpose   To make a child aware of his body and space through the conscious use of his visual system and the simultaneous movement of his arms in alternation with the simultaneous movement of his legs.

equipment   Colored paper stickers or childrens' "tattoo" transfers.

set up

1   Have the child affix a sticker or tattoo to the back of each hand. The letter "R" should appear on the right hand; the letter "L" on the left. The letters should read right-side-up, as illustrated.

2   Ask the child to affix the two letters to his knees in the same manner. These letters should also read right-side-up, as illustrated.

3   Ask the child to assume the creeping position, with his hands approximately seven inches in front of his knees, and his hands and knees each about twelve inches apart.

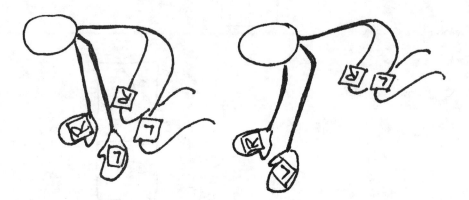

procedure

1   The child moves both hands forward simultaneously, looking at them as he does so, and calling out "hands."

2   The child looks at his knees, and with his weight resting on his hands, moves his knees forward together, calling out "knees."

3   The child creeps the length of the room (12-16 feet, if possible), **calling out "hands, knees, hands, knees," etc., as he moves the appropriate limbs.** Watch to see that he observes his hands and knees as he calls them, that his hands remain the same distance apart as his knees, that his movement is smooth and rhythmic.

4   The child creeps backward, "steering with his knees." He watches his knees and hands as he moves them, calling out "knees, hands, knees, hands," etc.

5   He continues to creep forward and backward for approximately five minutes.

keys to improvement

1   The arms move simultaneously.

2   The legs move simultaneously.

3   Visual fixation shifts smoothly from hands to knees and from knees to hands.

4   Both forward and backward creeping are smooth and rhythmic.

Figure 1a.

awareness level creeping: alternate side

purpose To make a child aware of his body and space through the conscious use of his visual system and the simultaneous movement of his right arm and right leg in alternation with the simultaneous movement of his left arm and left leg.

equipment Colored paper stickers or childrens' "tattoo" transfers.

set up

1 The stickers or tattoo transfers should be affixed to the child's hands and knees as in procedure **a**.

2 Ask the child to assume a creeping position with his left hand and left knee approximately seven inches in front of his right hand and right knee, respectively. In this position his left hand will be about fourteen inches ahead of his right knee.

procedure

1 Looking at the target on his right hand, the child moves his right hand and right leg forward simultaneously about fourteen inches, calling out the word "right" as he does so.

2 The child shifts his eyes to the target on his left hand and calls out the word "left" as he moves his left hand and left leg forward simultaneously.

3 The child creeps the length of the room (twelve to sixteen feet, if possible) calling out "right, left, right, left" etc., as he moves each side of his body. Upon reaching the end of the room, he reverses direction and returns to his starting point in the same manner.
Watch to see that he observes the appropriate hand as he moves it, and that his movement is smooth and coordinated, with his arms and legs moving forward simultaneously. They should both be lifted, and both hit the floor, at the same instant.

4 When the child has developed reasonable skill in creeping forward, **he** then creeps backward, again moving one side of his body at a time. When creeping backward he looks at his knee rather than his hand and continues to call out "right" and "left" as he moves.

5 The child creeps forward in one direction and backward in the other for approximately five minutes.

6 As the child's creeping becomes more coordinated, procedures **a, b,** and **c** of **awareness level creeping** will be intermixed. The method of intermixing the procedures is explained in procedure **c** of this unit—**cross body creeping.**

keys to improvement

1 The arm and leg move simultaneously as a unit.

2 Creeping is smooth and rhythmic both forward and backward.

3 Visual fixation is shifted accurately from hand to hand and knee to knee.

4 The head moves evenly with neither up nor down, nor side to side motion.

Figure 1b.

awareness level creeping: cross body

purpose
To make a child aware of his body and space through the conscious use of his visual system and the integrating demand of a cross-pattern movement.

equipment
Colored paper stickers or childrens' "tattoo" transfers.

set up

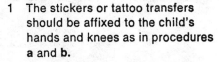

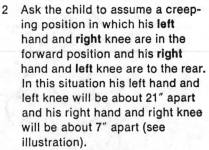

1 The stickers or tattoo transfers should be affixed to the child's hands and knees as in procedures **a** and **b.**

2 Ask the child to assume a creeping position in which his **left** hand and **right** knee are in the forward position and his **right** hand and **left** knee are to the rear. In this situation his left hand and left knee will be about 21″ apart and his right hand and right knee will be about 7″ apart (see illustration).

procedure

1 Looking at the target on his right hand, the child moves it and his left leg forward simultaneously, calling out "right hand" as he does so.

2 The child shifts his eyes to the target on his left hand and calls out "left hand" as he moves it and his right leg forward simultaneously.

3 The child creeps the length of the room in this manner, alternately calling out "right hand" and "left hand". Upon reaching the end of the room he reverses direction and returns to his starting point. Watch to see that his movement is smooth and coordinated, with simultaneous movement of the correct arms and legs.

4 When the child has developed reasonable skill in creeping forward, he then creeps backward in the cross body manner. When creeping backward he looks at his knee rather than his hand, calling out "right leg" or "left leg" as he moves it. The hand on the side opposite the knee moves backward in unison.

5 The child alternates creeping forward and backward for approximately five minutes.

6 When the child has become proficient in each of the three fundamental creeping patterns—bilateral, alternate side, and cross body—the challenges should be intermixed. For example: forward, cross body; backward, alternate side; forward, bilateral; backward, cross body, etc. (Several training sessions employing each of the three patterns separately will be necessary before most children are ready to handle the intermixing.)

keys to improvement

1 The arm and leg move simultaneously as a unit.

2 Creeping is smooth and rhythmic both forward and backward.

3 Visual fixation is shifted accurately from hand to hand, and knee to knee.

4 The head moves evenly with neither up nor down or side to side motion.

Figure 1c.

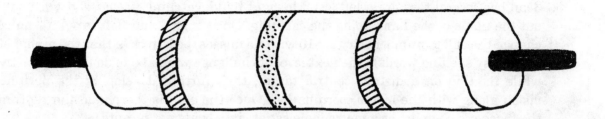

Illustration 4.

bend right knee while pushing down on left leg and straightening left knee. Then bend left knee while straightening right knee, and so on. This is done to rhythm provided by metronome set at sixty beats per minute or teacher's clapping, with student verbally reinforcing by calling name of straightened leg. Student looks at target specified by teacher. (Place a red paper "X" on the opposite wall, at child's chin level.)

4. *Marsden ball*[3] suspended from ceiling on nylon fishing line; tap with rolling pin held chest-high with one hand on each end; legs apart, with non-dominant foot forward. By banding the pin first with various colors of adhesive cloth tape, the task becomes more specific and challenging (see Illustration 4). For example, "Hit the ball on the green line ten times, then the yellow-right or yellow-left ten times, etc." A strong cardboard roll from paper towels may be substituted for the rolling pin. Any ball about 3 inches in diameter may be used. There are various ways to attach the nylon string. If the ball is solid, a long, "eye" type screw can be threaded through it, secured by a nut. If the ball is hollow, a large paper clip can be partially straightened, forced through, then turned again with a pliers, and forced back in.

The balls already prepared for stringing are available.

The Marsden ball is also used to develop smooth eye movements which help the child to read across a line of print, eliminating extraneous eye movements which can cause skipping of words or lines (see "Visual pursuits," page 97).

5. *Bean bag*[4] toss: use preferred hand, tossing first into small waste basket or box, then at masonite clown with holes cut out or whatever target is available. Bean bags should be small and light enough to fit comfortably in child's hand. They can be made easily from scraps of sturdy fabric, such as corduroy or denim, and filled with rice. Make several different sizes and let child practice with them until he decides which works best for him. Have child start close enough to get the bag into the receptacle.

---

[3] *Marsden ball,* developed by optometrist Carl D. Marsden from Colorado. To use this ball most efficiently, attach it to a nylon fishing line which is then threaded through an eye-screw in the ceiling or above a doorway. The ball can be pulled up and the string wrapped around a cleat on the wall when it is not in use. This set-up provides flexibility as to the height of the ball, since each person using it for batting must have it adjusted to meet his requirements. Keep in mind that the space needed for swinging the ball will be approximately 4 feet. Marsden balls may be ordered (*see* Sources).

[4] *See* Sources.

Then ask him to take one step away and try again. Keep the challenge realistic and achievable. Bean bags may also be purchased.

6. Bean bag lateral toss: from left hand to right hand, catching it securely, while calling out the name of the hand doing the catching. Once "right" and "left" are internalized, change the call to numbers (try for 10 with no misses) or letters (either the alphabet or some easy spelling words). The next level of challenge would be to do the same activity while fixating on a distant central target, thus further developing the peripheral vision along with the motor coordination. Once the skill is there, add the rhythm of the teacher's clapping or a metronome set at sixty beats per minute.

7. Bounce and catch an 8-inch playground ball. Start with a simple "drop-and-catch." Have child stand with feet about 12 inches apart, holding ball with both hands. After several successful experiences at this activity, gradually build to "drop, push down, and catch" (2 bounces). Continue to give plenty of opportunity to practice this while increasing the number of bounces, counting aloud or saying the A,B,C's. When secure with two-handed bouncing, have him try one hand at a time, alternating. Then let him try just one hand for five bounces and the other for five. Advanced level bouncing is with two balls simultaneously, with verbal distraction such as simple math computations, i.e., "2 + 2 = __." Maintain visual fixation between balls.

8. Toss ball against a wall (without windows) and catch it as it rebounds, with and without a bounce. Bounce/toss to partner and catch as she returns it. Count each successful catch, aiming for ten, then try "Hit the Disk." Place a colorful plastic chip about an inch in diameter, or a shiny coin on the floor. Keep track of how many times each hits the target with the ball. "Ten" usually wins. When doing the tossing, we teach the child to hold the ball with two hands in front of her chest, rather than over her head. This way she can keep her visual attention on the target, and is more apt to succeed.

9. Games such as dodge ball, kickball, soccer, stickball, "sticky ball" (the Velcro mitts with fuzzy ball), volleyball, ring toss, ping-pong, badminton, tennis, croquet, ten pins (bowling), softball, as well as all varieties of "tag" are to be encouraged as they develop eye-hand and eye-foot coordination, awareness, and experience with movement through space.

10. Clapping games (hands together, hands to partner's, right hands clap, left hands clap, repeat building speed). Usually accompanied by a sing-song chant.

11. Develop finger strength and dexterity with these exercises:

   A. Clay play includes pinching, rolling, pulling, squeezing, molding.

   B. Pinch clothespins open, set them on the edge of an empty cardboard box or coffee can, then pinch them off again and drop them into the container. Use one hand at a time for pinching and the other for holding the container, then switch hands and do it again. Awareness that the body is two-sided, and that one side is usually stronger is graphically illustrated by this activity. This procedure also demonstrates that the "weaker" side helps the "stronger." Make sure the child is using his thumb and pointer fingers only, rather than a group of fingers, or the pointer will not develop the strength it needs.

   C. Playing scales on a piano or keyboard.

   D. Typing on typewriter or computer.

    E. Finger painting.

    F. Origami.

    G. Cutting and pasting chains of colored paper or collages.

12. Jumping rope, with feet together is a skill that requires coordination between arms/hands, legs/feet, and eyes plus timing. If the child has had no prior experience, try the demonstration technique first, if you can, or get a good rope-jumper to demonstrate for you. Then give the novice lots of encouragement and time for practice with a rope that is not too long or too short. Some boys think that jumping rope is only for girls. These are the ones you'll need to show pictures of prize fighters in training and other athletes jumping rope to develop their leg and arm muscles as well as their general coordination. Heinsen considers jumping rope important enough to assign it three levels of procedures with very careful directions (see Figures 7a, 7b, and 7c).

As you begin to work with some of these techniques, variations will occur to you. You may feel more comfortable with some than with others. There is no hard and fast rule that must be followed other than to remember the purpose of the work you are doing with the children: you and they are striving for good motor coordination as a foundation for learning and the eyes lead the way.

FINE MOTOR ACTIVITIES

Many people don't realize that their eyes can be taught to work more efficiently. Since the muscles which control the movement of the eyes are not visible, most people don't even think about them. My awareness of the importance of eye movements was heightened through my association with my husband, Dr. Stanley H. Levine, a developmental optometrist, and his colleagues. Some of the pioneers in the field of children's vision did considerable research and prepared programs to be taught in public and private schools to enhance children's ability to learn by developing specific eye movement patterns. In *Developing Learning Readiness*, Getman and his associates described specific activities to develop these fine motor skills. In *Visual Motor Development*, Heinsen described other procedures which are also effective in developing attentional skills. Both of these programs have been utilized in the Child Development Program at John Adams School successfully. The Getman program has been used consistently in our kindergartens since 1973 as a preventive measure, with all the children participating. The Heinsen program has been used mainly in small groups and with individuals at all our grade levels since it was first made available to schools in 1974.

Section IV of *Developing Learning Readiness* deals exclusively with eye movements. *Saccadic* movement is the ability to change eye fixation from one point to another. *Pursuit* is the ability of the eyes to follow a moving target.

Here are some of the procedures for developing efficient *saccadic* movements:

1. Have children stand next to their seats, extending both arms forward from their shoulders, thumbs up on each hand. We ask them to hold a green crayon in the left fist, a red crayon in the right. Holding their heads still, with noses pointed straight ahead, they are to look at the green crayon, then the red, then back to the green without

jump rope 1

purpose

To further develop the child's ability to direct the movement of his body in a bilateral manner, and his ability to visualize the location of an object in time and space.

equipment

Jump rope.

procedure

step one

1 Ask the child to hold one end of the rope in each hand, allowing enough slack so that the rope dangles on the floor when his hands are held waist high.

2 Ask the child to look at the rope as he steps over it with his right foot first, and then with his left foot first. He should repeat this a few times.

3 The child should next look at some point in the distance at about eye level as he steps back and forth over the rope a few times. Ask the child to visualize the rope as he does so.

4 Begin to direct the child, each time he steps over the rope, to lead with a specific foot.

5 Give the child short sequences to remember, and follow with his feet, e.g., left, right, left, left, right.

6 Ask the child to lay the rope on the floor in a snake pattern. Have the child tiptoe through the pattern forward, then backward. He should do this first looking at a point straight ahead, then, when you feel he is ready, with his eyes closed.

step two

1 Ask the child to again hold the rope slack in each hand, but now to hop with **both feet together** forward and backward over the rope. Instruct him to look at the rope at first and then, as his proficiency increases, to look at a fixation point straight ahead and, finally, to carry out the activity with his eyes closed.

2 Have him again lay out the snake pattern, but this time to hop with both feet on tiptoe forward and backward. He should first fixate upon a point straight ahead and later carry out the activity with his eyes closed.

step three

1 Holding the rope in each hand, the child moves it back and forth in a pendulum motion. He is to hop with both feet together at the right time so that the rope moves forward and back freely under his feet.

2 As the child's proficiency increases, he should begin to fixate on a point in the distance as he carries out this activity, and, finally, do it with his eyes closed.

We suggest that the child practice **jump rope** for approximately ten minutes per training session. In the beginning, for many children, these ten minutes will be devoted entirely to **jump rope 1**, later to **jump rope 2** and, finally, to **jump rope 3.** It is important to keep in mind the fact that the three **jump rope** procedures form a hierarchy, and that the child should progress from one to another only when you believe him to be ready, based upon your observation of his proficiency.

keys to improvement

1 The child demonstrates that he knows the location of the rope in time and space without directly observing it.

2 The child performs all of the activities smoothly, and with rhythm.

Figure 7a.

jump rope 2

purpose To further develop the child's ability to direct the movement of his body in a bilateral manner, and his ability to visualize the location of an object in time and space.

equipment Jump rope.

set up Select a location where the rope can be swung freely, and tie one end of the rope to some object about three feet high.

procedure
step one

1 You or a helper turn the rope slowly and smoothly in a full circle for the child. Ask him to hop over it with both feet at a time, while looking ahead at a spot 6 yards away on the horizon. The child should try to be aware of as much of his surroundings as possible while looking at the fixation point. Instruct him to visualize the rope as it turns, and his feet as he hops over the rope.

2 When the child's hopping appears skillful, the rope should be turned in the opposite direction so that he must hop over it backwards.

step two

1 As above, but now hopping over the rope one foot ahead of the other. The child should practice leading with one foot for a while then the other.

2 The child should continue to look at the fixation point, at the same time trying to be aware of as many things in his field of view as possible.

3 When the child is able to carry out the above activities with rhythm and grace, ask him to try to rotate clockwise and counterclockwise while hopping.

keys to improvement

1 The child begins to jump rope with fewer misses and improved balance.

2 The child is able to continue jumping while observing his surroundings with his side vision.

3 The child progresses to the more difficult steps, while maintaining smoothness and rhythm.

Figure 7b.

jump rope 3

purpose To further develop the child's ability to direct the movement of his body in a bilateral manner, and his ability to visualize the location of an object in time and space.

equipment Jump rope.

set up Select an area in which the child can swing the rope freely.

procedure

step one 1 Ask the child to turn the rope slowly and smoothly over his head while hopping over it with both feet at a time. He should be fixating on a point ahead, and trying to be aware of as much of his surroundings as possible.

2 As the child develops proficiency in this activity he should begin to carry it out while turning the rope backwards.

step two 1 The child carries out the above activities leading with one foot at a time. He should practice leading with the right foot for a while, then with the left foot.

2 He hops forward and backward, continuing to fixate on a point ahead of him while remaining aware of other things in his field of view.

step three 1 When the child is able to carry out this activity with rhythm and grace, ask him to move forward to a fixed spot while skipping, and backward to his starting place.

2 The child repeats this activity turning the rope backwards.

3 When you feel the child is ready, ask him to rotate clockwise and counterclockwise while jumping rope.

4 Allow the child to make a second skip between hops. This will enable him to create a more rhythmic pattern in his jumping.

keys to improvement 1 The child is able to jump rope with fewer misses with better balance.

2 The child is able to keep the rope going as he observes his surroundings with his side vision, and is able to see more things at one time.

3 The child accomplishes the more difficult steps successfully, with smoothness and rhythm.

Figure 7c.

letting their heads move (see *Developing Learning Readiness*, page 69 for continued instructions).

2. Practice in saccadic movements directs the children to look at targets on the chalkboard as presented, first on the left, then on the right. While the children are performing these activities, the teacher must monitor their eye movements, and give them sufficient practice to determine that all have succeeded at this level (*Developing Learning Readiness*, page 70).

3. Having accomplished the horizontal saccades (the easiest), the children are then directed through vertical, diagonal, and near-to-far eye movements using specific targets which are reproducible for "near" and large numerals or pictures on the board for "far" (*Developing Learning Readiness*, pages 70 through 74).

4. For extra practice (if needed for individuals), we have devised a few exercises such as the cat-ball (see Illustration 5) for younger children; for older students, letters down each side of the page that form a message when horizontal and diagonal saccades are performed accurately (see Illustrations 6 and 7).

5. On chalkboard, put five numerals or letters across top and another five across middle. Hand out pages with same configuration of familiar items (see Illustrations 8 and 9). Have children call out targets as they look at them, from near to far, left to right. By having the children verbalize what they are fixating on, the teacher can more easily monitor a whole group noting which children are saying what they should be saying, and which ones seem to be "lost." The latter group needs to have more individual practice.

6. *Sensory-system-matching* exercises (see following page 19 in Chapter 2) better known to the graduates of our Child Development Program as the "Oink-quack-up-down-right-left" exercises have long been a delightful challenge in saccadic eye movement. Having used it for whole classes (with the overhead projector) as well as for small groups and individuals in remedial sessions, we can wholeheartedly endorse this valuable activity. It helps children learn to stay on line, developing accuracy and speed in reading, in a thoroughly enjoyable manner. Remember to use the metronome in the final stages of these activities, set at sixty beats per minute, and increasing speed to 120. Adding the "beat" to any of these activities helps to establish the total organization of the person accomplishing the task. The title of this group of exercises could be paraphrased : See it, interpret it, say it, and do it, matching the audible stimulus.

7. *Ann Arbor Tracking Programs,*[5] beginning with Symbol Tracking, and extending through Letter Tracking and Word Tracking are excellent, available, and have also withstood the tests of time. The basic activity upon which these programs are based is that of scanning across a line of symbols, searching for a specific item. Once found, a mark is made on or around the item, and then the eyes must continue seeking the next targeted item. Ann Arbor offers a wide variety of which we suggest the reader begin with the three mentioned above, in reproducible form. Be sure to record each child's time on his effort, and chart it for at least twenty pages (2 pages a day is sufficient) to show him and his parents how much he has improved his tracking skills. No need to do endless drills; start the next level of challenge.

[5] *See* Sources.

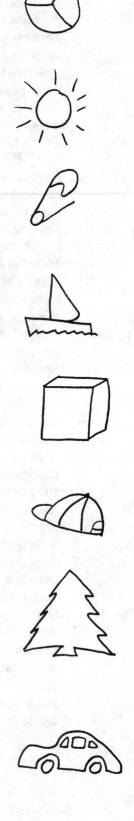

Illustration 5.

Illustration 6.

Illustration 7.

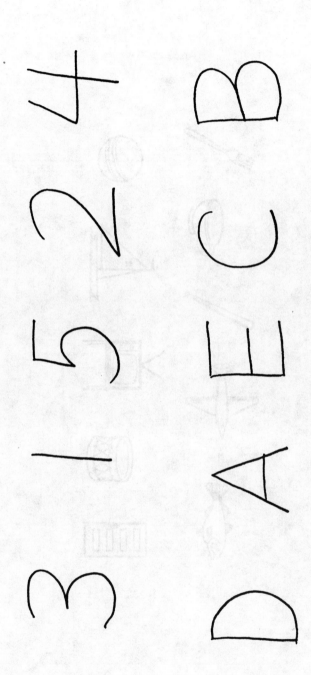

Illustration 8.

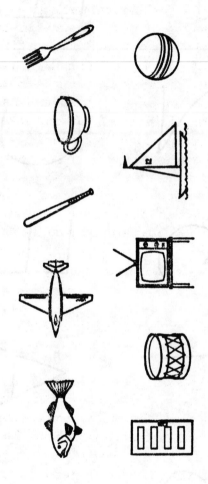

Illustration 9.

To develop smooth *visual pursuits:*

1. Follow instructions with Space Sighters on page 75 of *Developing Learning Readiness* (use large wands from bubble liquid).

2. Have child lie on the floor. If not carpeted, use a small mat under his head and back. The Marsden ball is suspended about 16 inches above the center of his chest. The child should be relaxed, his feet slightly apart, his arms at his sides, and his head straight. Set the ball in motion, so that it circles slowly over the child, and ask him to follow the ball with his eyes. The teacher or a helper must monitor the student's eye movements while he follows twenty times clockwise and then twenty times counterclockwise. The student should be able to maintain these circular movements without losing visual contact with the ball. If his eyes stray from their target, he must be told each time it happens. There should be no movement of the head, only the eyes. At first, it may be very difficult for him to accomplish this task. If so, ask him to point his finger at the ball while he looks at it, and this will help him to maintain his gaze. For variety, you can swing the ball horizontally, vertically, or diagonally. Smooth eye movements are the goal of this exercise; it may take several attempts before he becomes successful, but keep encouraging him to put forth the effort. Ideally, this exercise should first be done one eye at a time, with the other eye covered by an eye patch. A clean folded tissue can serve that purpose. Once the child is successful with smooth monocular eye movements, you can ask him to continue the activity and at the same time, count or spell simple words or carry on a conversation. Then have him review the same procedures using both eyes. This exercise, properly executed, will develop the skills the child needs to read without losing his place on the page. An extended use of this procedure, to develop peripheral awareness is: while maintaining his fixation on the moving ball, the student should be able to answer questions about other things in his visual field, such as, "What color crayon am I holding?" or "What shape is this block?"

3. *Controlled Reader*[6] — develops smooth left-to-right eye movements, with adjustable speeds. Filmstrip material varies: start with reading matter below child's actual level and progress to more difficult vocabulary.

4. Following mazes: start on chalkboard. Take two chalks in one hand and draw a road on the board. Make the first one horizontal. Have children take turns following the road with a toy car or truck, then a piece of chalk. Gradually increase the complexity of the road by adding hills and valleys. Next have them try to follow the road using only their eyes, and not moving their heads. Draw several roads that overlap, twist and turn, and have the children try to follow one road at a time, visually (see Illustrations 10 and 11). Follow with commercially available mazes for extra practice.

5. Follow the marble around the pie pan: keeping head still, move only the eyes. Must be monitored by teacher or partner. Child holds the pie pan at chin level in front of him, tilting the pan slightly so that the marble will roll steadily around the edge of the pan. Child watches the marble, counting its trips around the circle. A realistic goal is ten clockwise and ten counterclockwise, without "breaking", i.e., losing eye contact with the marble. Encourage development of slow, steady rhythm.

---

[6] Also known as Guided Reader, this equipment may already be in your school's reading laboratory in middle school or even at the high school, where it has been used in remedial programs. If your search for it proves fruitless, the Guided Reader is now available for use with computers (*see* Sources).

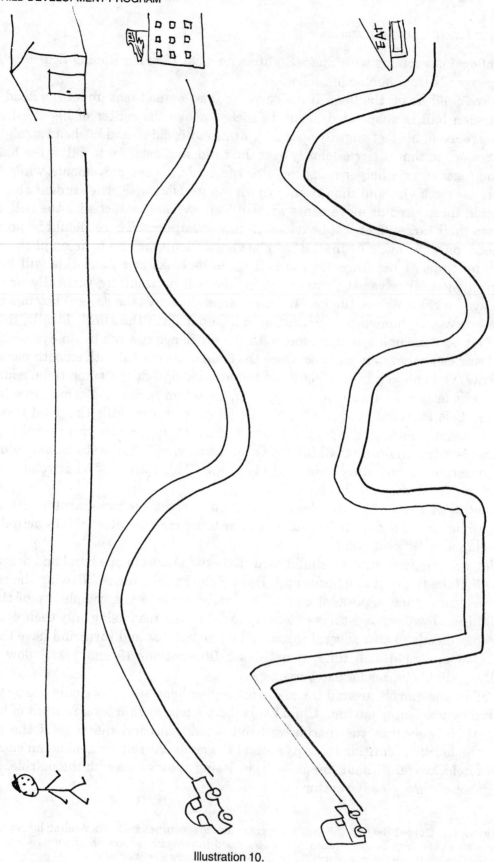

Illustration 10.

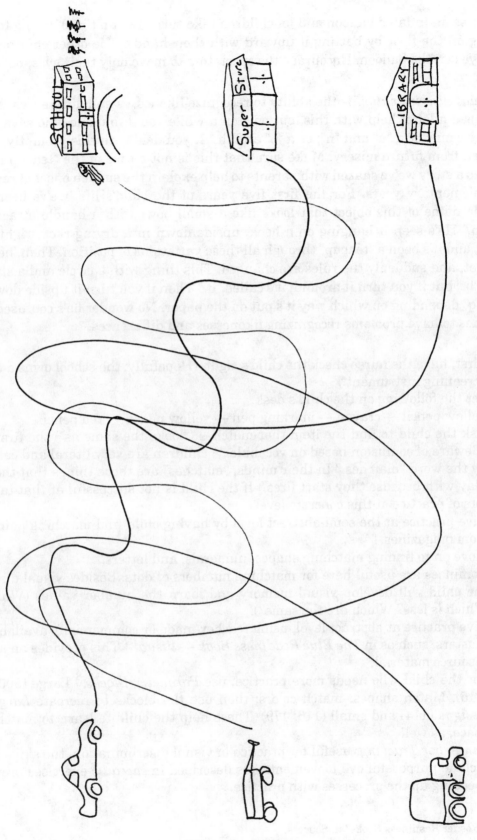

Illustration 11.

6. Use an inflated balloon and let children take turns (2 at a time), trying to keep it from landing on the floor by batting it upward with their hands. The other children are to keep their eyes on the balloon. Encourage the spectators to move only their eyes, not their heads.

Visual discrimination is the ability to recognize likenesses and differences. Most children don't need a lot of help with this, but once in a while you'll find one who says a "b" and "d" look the same; or a "u" and "n"; or a "b" and "h." If you deal with this promptly, the child can be saved from future misery. Make sure that this is not a case of the "teacup mix-up." This refers to a story we've shared with parents to help explain the sudden onset of reversals in the early elementary years. For the first five years of the child's life, we've been telling him that the name of this object that looks like a small bowl with a handle attached to it is a "teacup." He's seen it hanging on a hook, upside down in a drying rack, rightside up on a saucer, and it's been a "teacup" through all these variations of position. Then, here comes the alphabet, and suddenly the rules are changed. This thing with a circle and a straight line is called "b," but if you turn it around, it's called "d." Then if you turn it upside down, it's called "p" or "q" depending on which way it's put on the paper. No wonder he's confused. If the child continues to have problems recognizing likenesses and differences,

1. First, have the nurse check the child's sight. (Hopefully, the school owns a telebinocular screening instrument.)
2. Set the following on the child's desk:
   yellow pencil — crayon — marking pen — yellow pencil — red pencil
   Ask the child to find the item that matches ("looks the same as") the first in the row. (Beware of confusion based on vocabulary: children are very literal and can be derailed by the word "matches." In their minds, "matches" are those things that they are not to play with because they start fires.) If the child is not successful at that task, he needs lots of practice at this concrete level.
3. Give practice at the semi-abstract level by having child find matching pairs of pictures from magazines.
4. Move on to finding matching shapes, numerals, and letters.
5. Dominoes are useful here for matching numbers of dots. Besides visual discrimination, the child will develop visual memory and learn the number values (Which is more? Which is less? Which are the same?).
6. Give practice at abstract level, using teacher-made or commercially available black-line masters, such as in *The Blue Readiness Book — Visual*.[7] This provides an abundance of resource material.
7. For the child who needs more practice, use *Parquetry Blocks*,[8] Large (500) and Small (115). Match shapes; match colors; then use the blocks to recreate *Large Parquetry Designs* (114) and small (116, 179). These help the child to learn to match position in space, as well.
8. *Ann Arbor Tracking*: useful for practice in visual discrimination, the skills learned also include purposeful eye movements, (as described in *saccadic* exercises previously) and speeding up the processes with practice.

[7] *See* "Rosner Readiness Books" in Sources.
[8] *See* Sources.

9. *Vu-Mate*[9] training is accomplished with an individual tachistoscope which flashes material at 1/10 second or faster. It is used with the *Vu-Mate Perceptual Accuracy Book*. It can also be used for training instant word recognition. *Vu-Mate Words Books* are available from the same source.

Just a few more words here regarding errors in visual discrimination which are commonly referred to as "reversals." Unless the awareness of the differences between left and right has been internalized, there is always a potential problem that will not be outgrown. There are plenty of adults who need to look at the ring on a finger before they can tell you which is their right hand. Chances are these adults still have trouble reading and following directions when looking at a map. They may not have developed to their fullest potential because someone in their formative years thought they would outgrow their confusion regarding "b" and "d." At John Adams School, the Child Development Program tries to make sure that every child learns (internalizes) which is left and which is right. The gross motor activities discussed earlier in this chapter, which are done routinely with every kindergartener, include specific items leading to this internalization. Sometimes one or two don't get it the first time through. We then ask these youngsters to point to the ceiling with their right hands for five minutes (first checking to be sure that they have the correct hand raised.) Pretty soon, they're asking if they may put their hands down. "Is your right arm getting tired?" we ask, knowing what the answer will be. "Just a little longer, keep that tired right arm where it is." After the longest five minutes in their experience, their kinesthetic memories have been programmed, and they rarely forget which is "right" after that. Even with their eyes closed, they'll be able to remember that temporary discomfort. Then we can use this experience as a building block to learn more things about left and right, not the least of which is that the letter "b" has the bat on the left and the ball on the right, while the "d" has a drum on the left and a stick on the right. So you see, those two letters aren't the same after all. The only thing that is the same about them is that they're made with circles and lines, but so are the "p" and the "q."

Visual memory activities are those which help children learn to recall what they have seen. This skill is essential for success in reading, spelling, and math.

1. *Visual Memory Cards*[10] *Set II (181B)* and *Set III (182)* have proven to be extremely worthwhile when used as directed. Each box contains a series of stimulus cards and a set of response cards. The response cards are spread out in front of the child. The teacher holds the stimulus cards and shows one of them to the child for a few seconds. Using his response cards, he is to pull down only the pictures he saw on the stimulus card. The teacher shows the card again, and the child checks his work. If they match, he earns a point. Depending on the child's age and level of performance, we set the limits: usually five or ten points makes the "game," and the child gets to do a special activity as a reward. These cards can also be used to develop auditory memory, as described in Chapter 7.

2. *Sequential Picture Cards I (127)*[11] have given excellent value: their varied uses include developing visual memory, story writing, comprehension, and auditory memory. This particular set has been very popular with our students as the "stories," each told in six pictures,

[9] *See* Sources.

[10] *See* Sources.

[11] *See* Sources.

have special appeal. One deals with a little boy who falls off his bike, and another describes the getting-ready-for-bed routine of a little girl.

3. *Sight Word Lab I (637)*[12] can be used as a supplement to just about any reading program. It is easily used with individuals and small groups. When used as directed, it has proven very successful in helping children to master 200 basic sight words.

4. *Sound Foundations Program I (256)*[13] is a word attack/spelling program based on a phonics approach. It provides convenient, systematic review of specific phonetic sounds, set up in a varied, programmed sequence for independent, self-paced study. It has worked well with small groups of first, second, and third graders in the Child Development Program.

5. *Spelling Cards:* teacher-made of construction paper or oak tag scraps, each card is 2″ × 6″. The following technique works very well with all ages, but is especially effective with older students (grades 3 through 6) who have been getting low grades in their spelling tests. When they see their marks jump from D's and C's to B's and A's, their self-esteem soars and you know they'll try to do it again next week. This is how it works:

A. Sitting next to student, have him dictate each word while he is looking at his spelling book. As he says the word, and spells it, the teacher prints or writes it in large, *bright red* letters, using a broad-tipped marking pen, and repeats the spelling aloud when she has finished the card.

B. When the cards for the week are complete, the child is to trace the letters with his finger, saying each word and spelling it aloud.

C. As he finishes tracing the word, he is to close his eyes, and try to see the after-image on the "little computer screen" inside his eyelids, simultaneously making the letters in the air or on the desk while saying them aloud once more. (After staring at bright red for 10 seconds, close your eyes, and you will see the same image in green.)

D. Have the student open his eyes and trace the card once more, saying the letters aloud.

E. Then he turns the card over and prints or writes the word in his notebook.

F. Turn back to the card to check the word. If correct, give it a star; if incorrect, print or write it correctly from the card next to the first effort. Draw a line through the incorrect version.

G. Study all words that have not earned the star, and try them again the next day.

H. When all words have been mastered, ask him to spell each word forward and backward orally. This will indicate whether the child can visualize them and has truly internalized them. If he is successful at this, he is practically guaranteed to remember them forever.

Visual-motor skills are the ones needed for good eye-hand coordination, and are generally essential for legible writing, printing, and all other activities normally done in school such as cutting, drawing, and typing at a computer. Most children develop these skills as they grow and have the opportunities to experiment either at home or in a day care/nursery school facility. For those whose skills have not developed adequately and are subsequently hampered when asked to print or cut, we offer activities designed to help.

1. "Playing with blocks" becomes a structured learning exercise when the child is given *Parquetry Blocks (500)* and the *Design Cards (114)*. The first instruction is simply to place

[12]*See Sources.*
[13]*See Sources.*

the blocks directly on the card to verify location, and then to construct the designs in front of the patterns, which the teacher checks for accuracy. The level of difficulty will increase gradually through the smaller blocks (*115*) and corresponding design cards (*116, 179*). *Color Cubes (110)*[14] and their *Designs in Perspective (112)* are useful as well.

2. *Pegs (129)*[15] and *Pegboards (128)* provide additional opportunities for grasping smaller items and using them to reproduce the *Pegboard Designs (150)*.

3. Sewing cards: we make our own from styrofoam plates (recycled from the local supermarket) which are easily punctured with a knitting needle and can be made in a variety of simple designs. Each child is given a large blunt needle already threaded and knotted, and time to work the needle and yarn through all the holes.

4. Weaving potholders on small metal looms can be a learning experience as well as providing the child with a self-esteem enhancing opportunity to make a gift for the home. Parents always enjoy the efforts of their children, especially when they are useful.

5. Bead stringing to copy patterns develops the same skills as the sewing cards with the added challenge of picking up the correct bead and getting the end of the string through the little hole. Start with simple patterns such as red-green-yellow square beads and ask them to repeat that pattern. Gradually increase complexity including different shapes as well as colors. Once the child correctly reproduces a pattern of beads, he will find it easier to reproduce a series of letters or numbers.

6. Colored rubber bands can be used to make designs on *Geoboards*.[16] There are many variations available for this activity. The design to be reproduced can be drawn on the chalkboard, further exercising the "near-far" focusing mechanisms; or verbal directions can be given such as, "Stretch your green rubber band from the top-left peg to the top-right peg. Then stretch your blue rubber band from the top-middle peg to the bottom-middle peg. Now, what capital letter do you have on your geoboard?"

7. *Pick-Up-Sticks*[17] require careful coordination of the fingers and eyes.

8. Cut-and-paste pictures offer a wide variety of activities and can be as simple or as complex as the child cares to attempt. The use of scissors can be a challenge to some youngsters who may have had no opportunity to practice, or may be developmentally delayed. There are now *Easy-Grip Scissors*[18] designed to be operated by holding a plastic loop in one hand and squeezing it. There are also scissors designed for the teacher's hand to hold along with the student's (4 finger holes) which come in right- and left-handed models. Many scissors are now designed to cut equally well when held in either hand. Be sure to teach the correct finger positions for efficient use of scissors (see page 43).

While we usually reserve the use of "Perception +" for our kindergarten program, we may have a first grader who has just moved into our district and can benefit from exposure to this very unique set of exercises. The original name of "Perception +" was Project:SEE — Specific Education of the Eye; it was designed specifically to develop the

[14]*See* Sources.

[15]*See* Sources.

[16]*See* Sources.

[17]*See* Sources.

[18]*See* "Scissors" in Sources.

visual skills, and we definitely can use it to develop motor control as well as hand-eye coordination.

Tracing designs and completing partially printed designs lead quite naturally to replicating them. There are many commercially available, or you can make them yourself. One of my favorite programs which is no longer available was called *Look and Write.* It was published by Educational Developmental Laboratories, who have very generously granted permission to reproduce parts of the original. This structured learning-to-print set of exercises follows, along with my own printing paper which I adapted from the EDL model (see Illustration 12). When all other methods have left a kindergartener still frustrated with his attempts at printing, this one works.

We have synthesized a 120-page workbook into the following eighteen black line masters (see [Illustration 12] following 18 pages). As preparation for working with them, the children must be introduced to the "window." Draw a 3-foot square window on the chalkboard. Take the time to establish the name for each line in the window, i.e., top, bottom, middle, left, right, middle, calling on the children to give the words. Then place a large dot (use contrasting color chalk) on one of the intersections and ask for the location to be identified, i.e., "top-left." Abbreviate "T-L" and put it on the chalkboard near that corner. Then make another large window on the board and ask for a volunteer to come up and put a big dot on the top-left corner of that one.

Continue in this manner until all nine intersecting points have been identified and labeled, including "middle-middle." Following this introduction, the children are ready to use the black line masters as presented, although not necessarily the same day. We've found that a ten-minute limit to an activity like this keeps interest keen and productivity high. So, the next day, after they have correctly placed their dots, they are to make the lines that will connect them. If you encourage them to make these lines from *top to bottom* and from *left to right,* there should be no confusion. The letters and numerals that follow are arrow-directed. When first forming a letter, have the children identify the starting point and the ending point as they trace the model on the left. Using the same directions, they are to continue across the line. Check for accuracy as they are working. The blank copy is for extra practice.

The original *Look and Write,* an eye-hand coordination workbook was the creation of Stanford E. Taylor and was published by Educational Developmental Laboratories, a division of McGraw-Hill Book Company, New York in 1965. It was designed to help beginning readers develop an awareness of spatial relationships, visual discrimination, and facility in writing. When used as directed, it introduces and develops the student's awareness of placement, direction and shape, and follows the use of "Perception +" at the kindergarten level.

The various procedures outlined above should serve only as a beginning. There are many more variations which will occur to the user of the Child Development Program. The only basic rule to remember is: If what you are doing with the child is helping him to achieve success in his classroom, on the playground and at home, then you have accomplished your goal. If it has not, re-examine his needs and your efforts to meet them. Is there something else to be tried? Discuss your findings with your in-school committee (usually consisting of the principal, the nurse, the classroom teacher, and sometimes a member of the Special Services Child Study Team). It may be helpful to have a conference now with the parents to get more information about the child's performance at home. Look and listen for clues to help

Illustration 12.

Illustration 12. (Cont'd.)

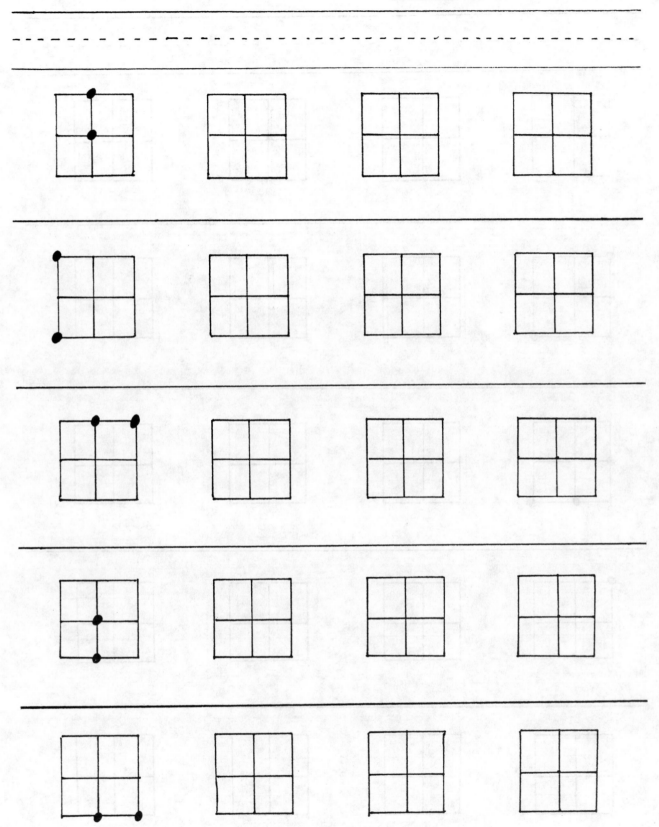

Illustration 12. (Cont'd.)

Illustration 12. (Cont'd.)

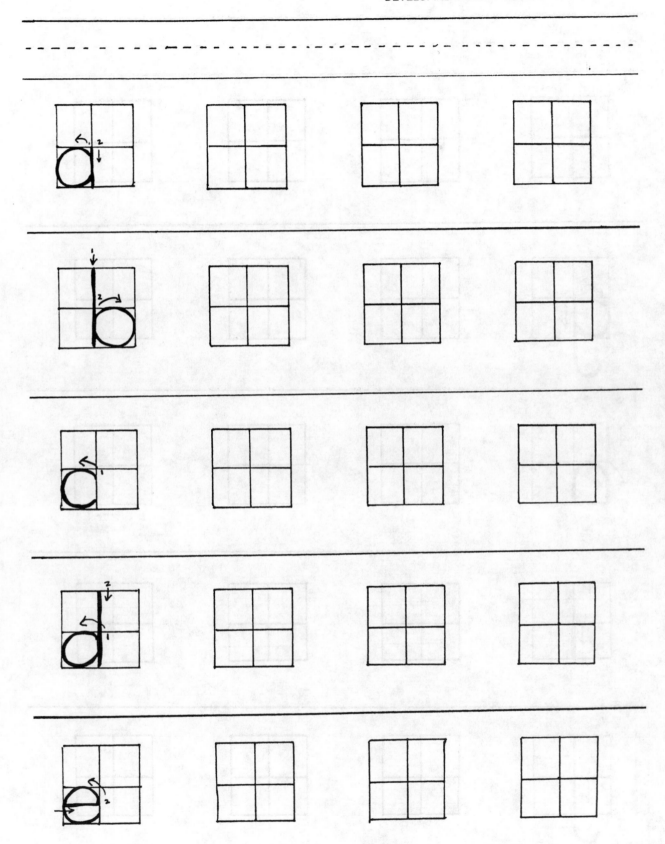

Illustration 12. (Cont'd.)

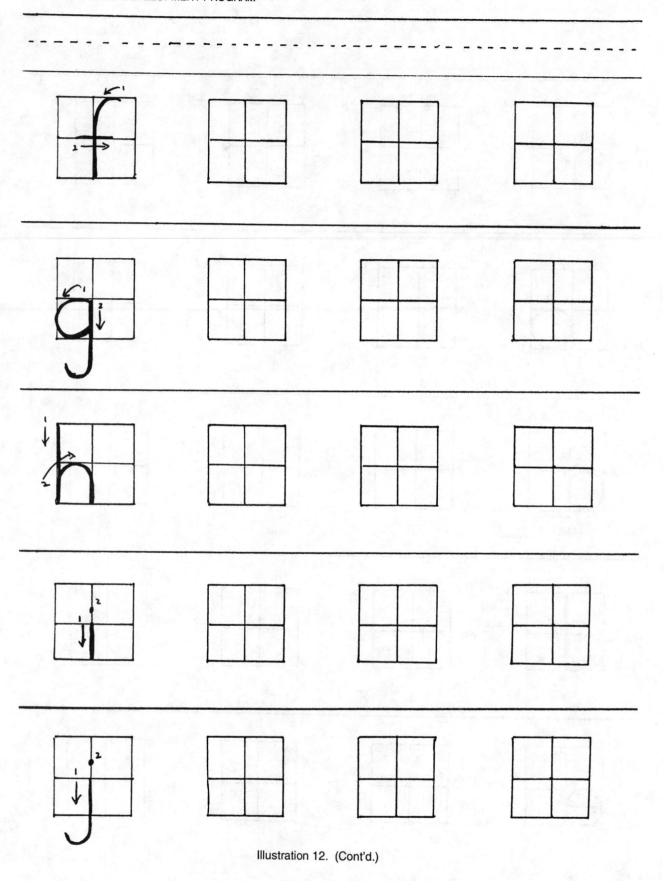

Illustration 12. (Cont'd.)

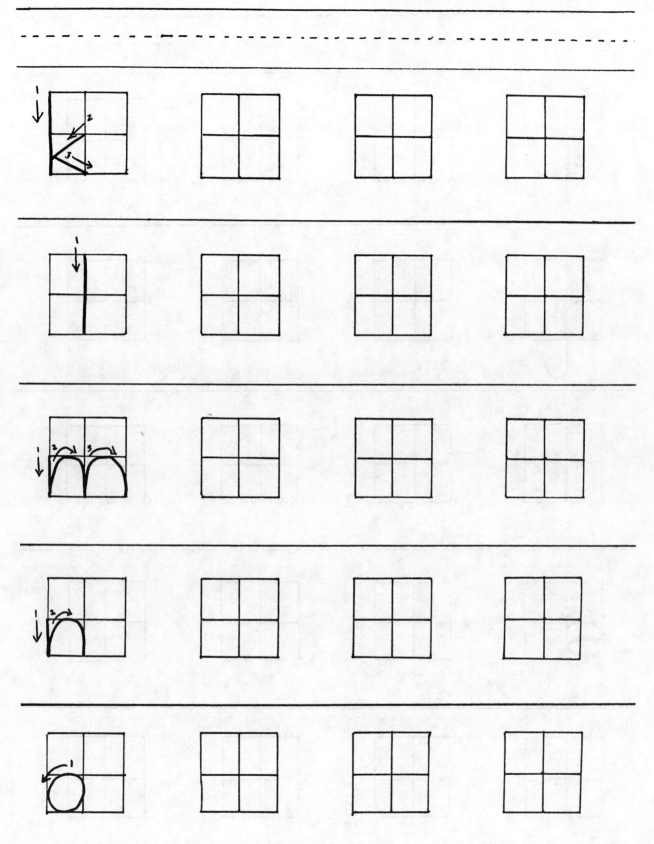

Illustration 12. (Cont'd.)

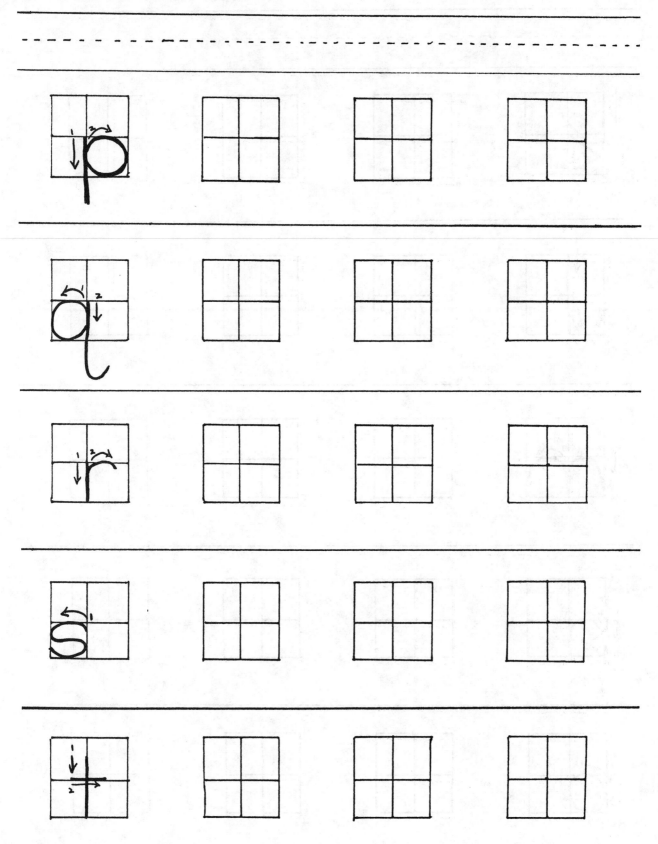

Illustration 12. (Cont'd.)

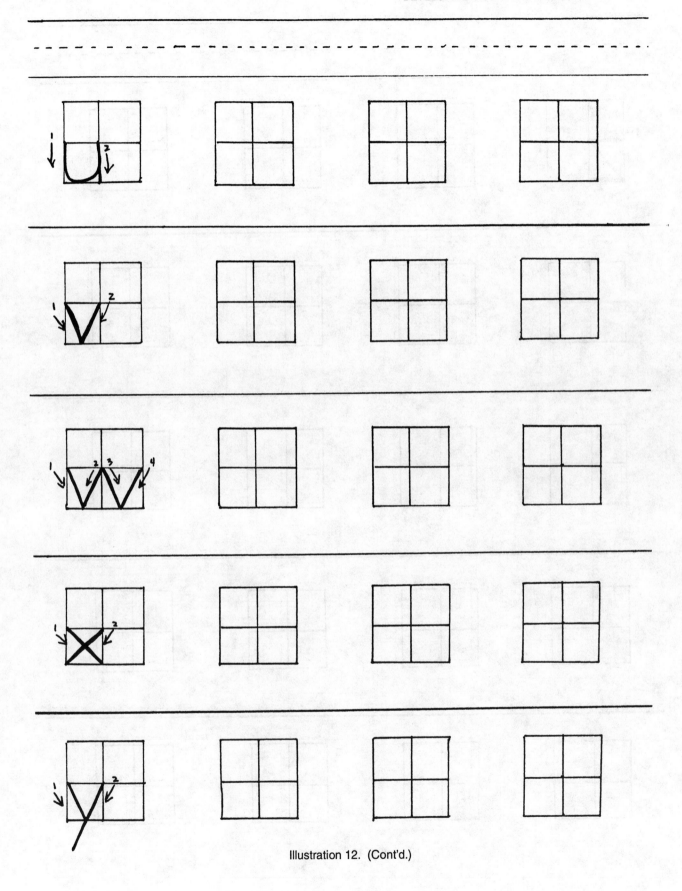

Illustration 12. (Cont'd.)

Illustration 12. (Cont'd.)

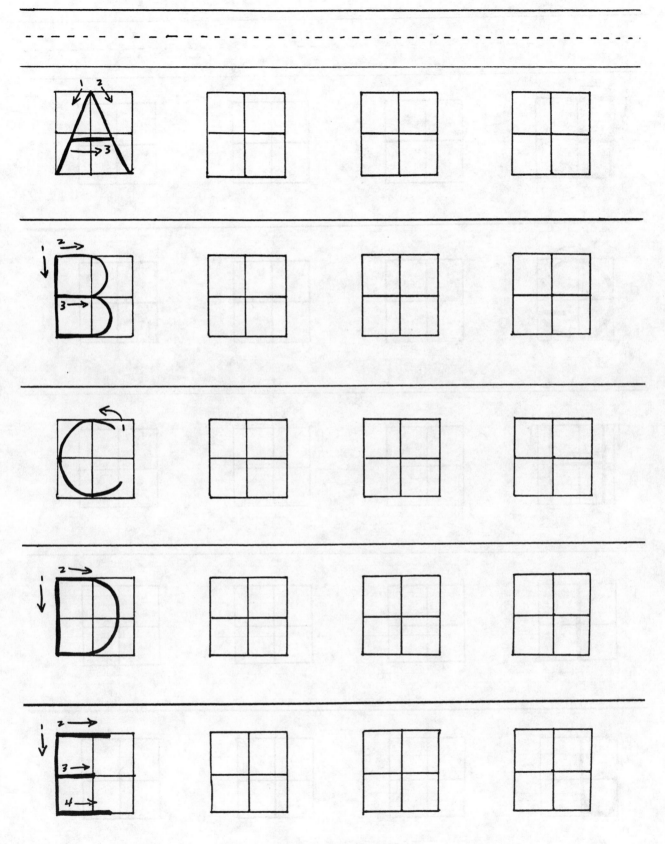

Illustration 12. (Cont'd.)

Illustration 12. (Cont'd.)

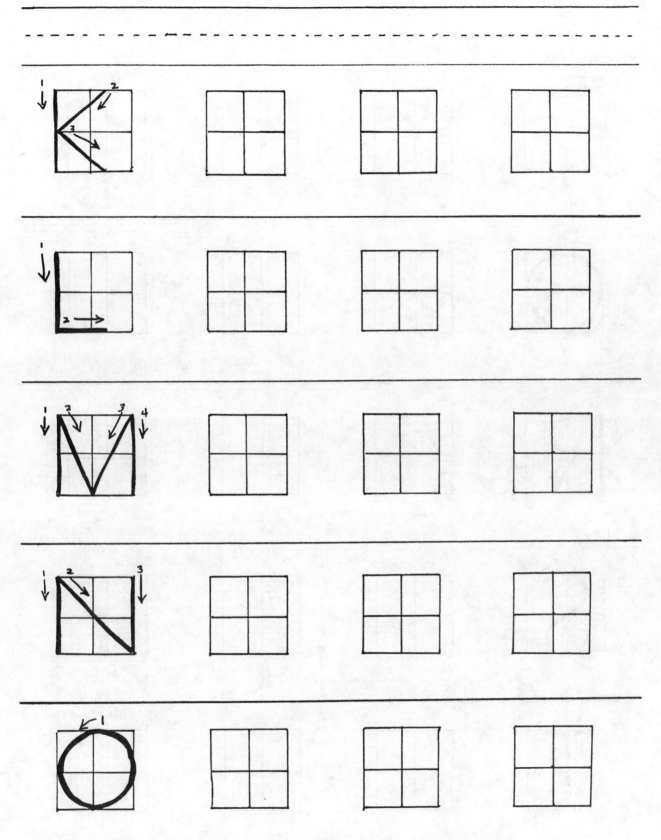

Illustration 12. (Cont'd.)

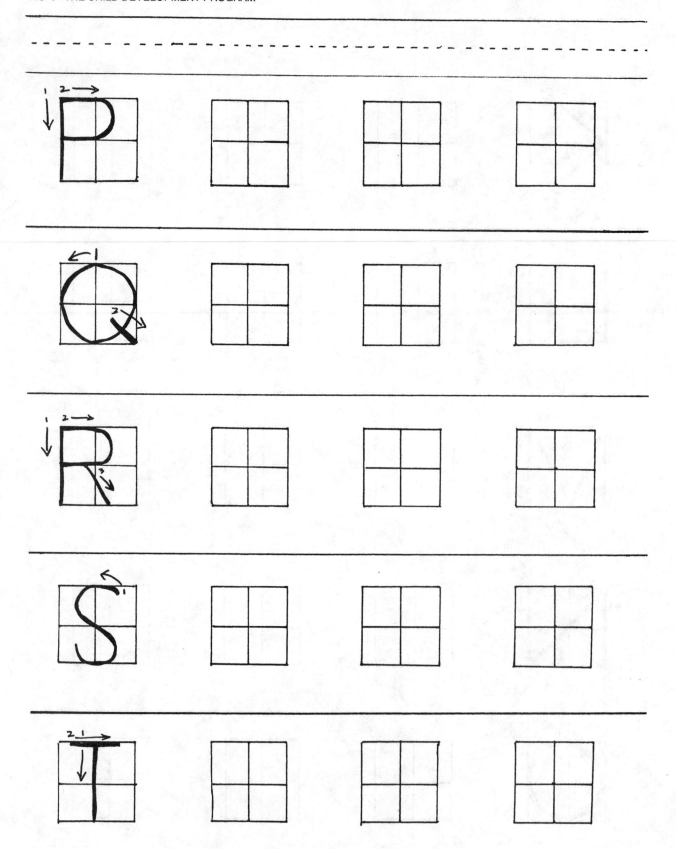

Illustration 12. (Cont'd.)

Illustration 12. (Cont'd.)

Illustration 12. (Cont'd.)

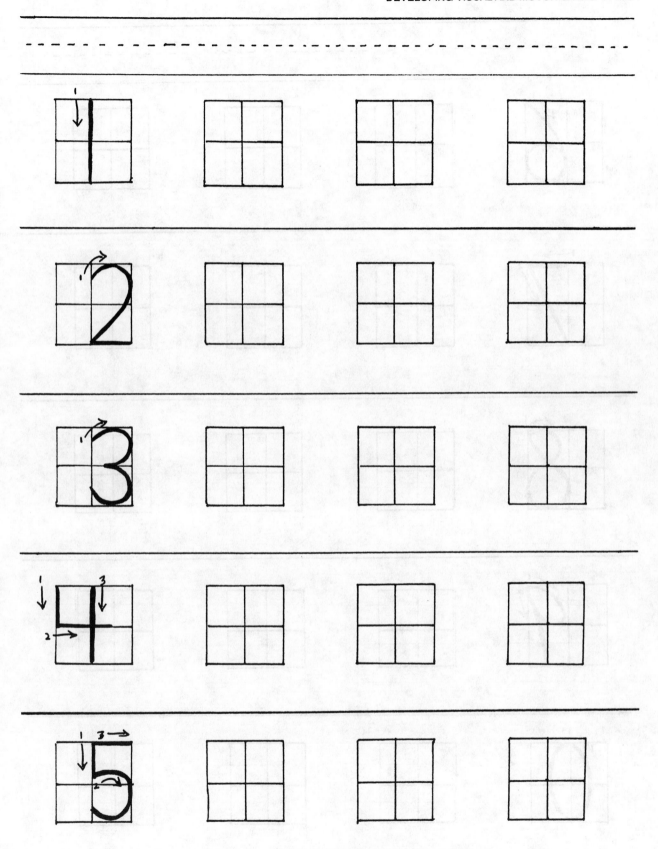

Illustration 12. (Cont'd.)

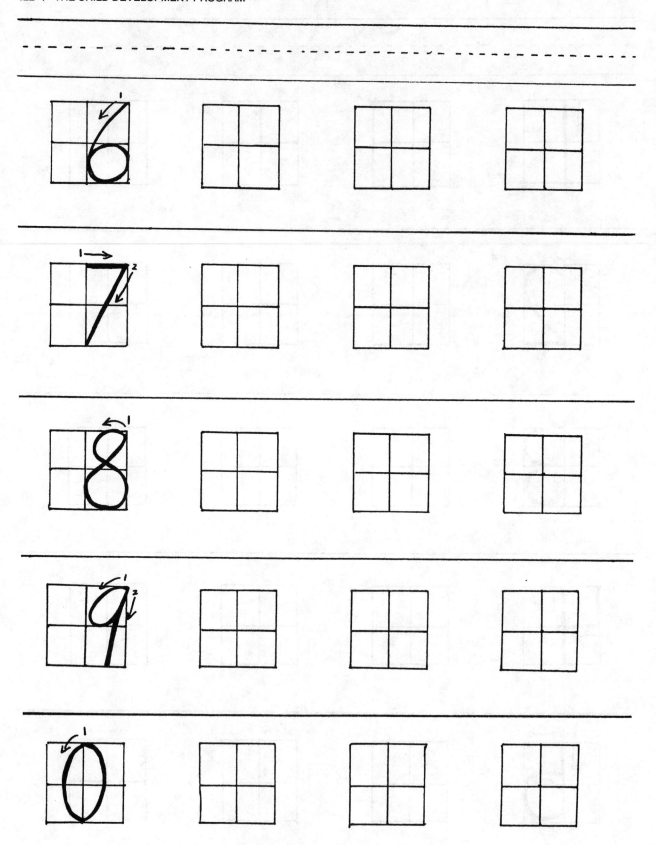

Illustration 12. (Cont'd.)

you find the key that will solve this child's problem. When all other avenues have been explored, it is my personal experience that leads me to suggest that the child be seen by a developmental optometrist. Sometimes a child can measure 20/20 in visual acuity and yet his eyes are not working together, as a team. It is usually the last specialist to see him, but the one that makes the most important discovery about him.

CHAPTER 7

Developing Auditory Skills

While most learning takes place visually, we are certainly aware of the importance of auditory skills. When a child seems not to be listening to the teacher, the first course of action is to ask the school nurse to do an audiometric screening to determine whether the child has a hearing impairment. Some children do suffer because of wax accumulation in their ears. More frequently, however, we find that the child can hear within normal ranges, but simply has not been paying attention to what the teacher has been saying. In this age, when radio and television are on all day in some households, it is a wonder that more children do not have auditory problems. Most have become skillful in selective listening and can "tune out" voices or sounds at will.

The next step is to assess the child's functioning with the use of the *Test of Auditory Perceptual Skills*.[1] Seven separate areas are included in the testing which when scored gives a clear picture of the youngster's auditory perceptual development. In the areas in which the child scored low, we proceed to encourage skill-building as follows.

AUDITORY DISCRIMINATION

1. Tape recording of common noises may be played for identification either verbally or by matching the sound heard with one of a group of pictures. *Listening Lotto-ry (EI-6158, -6159)*[2] or *Auditory Familiar Sounds (139)*[3] will help the child to "tune in" and make connections between auditory and visual.

2. Tap a ruler on the underside of the desk (out of sight) a specific number of times; have the children take turns responding with the number of taps heard. Teacher then holds up a card with the answer for immediate checking.

3. If *Buzzer Board* is available (it no longer appears in the catalog), it has two places to press and makes a buzzing sound. The teacher presses a signal, such as "Long — short — short," and the child returns the same message. A pack of cards with various numbers of dots and dashes accompanied the board, to verify the auditory message.

4. Use a musical instrument, such as a xylophone, to tap out a simple tune. Start with just a few notes and see if the child can recognize the melody and/or duplicate it. To sensitize listening skills, encourage singing along with the melody. When you use "Twinkle, Twinkle, Little Star," most children will join in.

[1] *See* Sources.
[2] *See* Sources.
[3] *See* Sources.

5. *Learning to Listen in the Classroom*[4] is a series of audiotapes. One entitled *Following Directions with Multi-Word Phrases (EI-6131)* trains the listener to focus on the voice and tune out the noisy backgrounds. The student is directed to respond by circling one of two pictures in each of ten boxes on the answer sheet. Twenty reproducible answer sheets accompany the tape. This program has had a high success rate in challenging the "selective listeners" and getting them to tune in more carefully to the classroom teacher.

6. *The Green Readiness Book-Auditory*[5] is packed with a variety of activities to build sound/symbol, decoding, and listening skills in the early elementary student.

AUDITORY MEMORY

Once we have them listening, we want them to remember what they have heard. Those who have trouble with this usually benefit from exercises to develop auditory memory. To set the stage and develop motivation, we ask these students to think about why it is important to remember precisely what we hear, such as names, phone numbers, addresses, directions, page numbers, etc. "What might happen if someone invited you to a party and you went to the wrong address?" "Suppose someone called with an important message for your parents and you wrote the phone number down in the wrong order?" Reaching closer to our point, "What if your teacher said you were going to have a test on page 12, but you forgot and studied page 20 instead." By this time, they are usually quite eager to practice auditory memory exercises.

1. With the younger children, we call this the "Polly Parrot" game: the teacher says a series of numbers, letters, or words into a tape recorder. The children take turns repeating the series into the recorder. Start with only two items, to insure success, and work up to five or six gradually. As the tape is played back, the numbers, letters, or words are placed on the board. Thus the children can check their responses visually, as well.

2. We get double usage from *Visual Memory Cards (181B)*[6] in this manner:
   a. Spread all response cards from one set on the desk in front of child.
   b. Keeping stimulus cards hidden from child, say the names of the pictures slowly in left to right order.
   c. Student then selects only the response cards called for and sets them in the same sequence.
   d. Teacher shows stimulus card to the student for checking.
   e. Helpful hint: when a child is having great difficulty with this task, say, "Close your eyes. Pretend you are looking at a TV or computer monitor. As you hear the names of these objects, the pictures are going to pop up on the screen in front of you. Now, open your eyes and find the cards that look just like the ones you saw on the inside of your eyelids." This technique usually works, and while some might argue that it doesn't belong with auditory skills because it is encouraging visualization, we use it because it teaches the child to be more successful at recalling what he has heard.

3. Use the alphabet as cues for remembering a list of objects with this "shopping game":
   Teacher: "I'm going to the store for apples."
   First student: "I'm going to the store for apples and bananas."

[4] *See* Sources.

[5] *See* Sources.

[6] *See* Sources.

Next student: "I'm going to the store for apples, bananas, and corn."

Continue in this manner, to the end of the alphabet.

4. "Telephone game" (works best with a group of 5 or 6 children): All sit in a circle. Teacher whispers a phrase or sentence from a card hidden in her hand to the first student on her left, who then whispers the same message to the next child, and so on around the circle. The last student says it aloud and the teacher records this on the chalkboard. Directly beneath it, teacher places original message from card. The group analyzes the changes, if any, and reviews need for accuracy in relaying messages. This is a good time to teach the importance of 911 calls and when to use that special easy-to-remember number.

5. *Auditory Perception Training—Memory (7171)*[7] is a program using audio tapes with reproducible worksheets. The first few lessons have just two pictures per row. The child is to work with them as directed by the narrator, who warns us that he may not always say things in the same order that they appear on the worksheet. The voice then names the objects, tells us which item to mark, in what manner, and which crayon to use. The challenge builds in manageable steps until the child is capable of retaining five items in the order given, with different colors and different types of marks for each row. We have had a great deal of success with this program.

6. Tell a story in three sentences. Place the sentences (each on a strip of oak tag) in a random pile on the student's desk. Child is to read them and set them in the order originally heard. This can work with numerals and letters also.

7. Tape record a story incorporating pictures of *Sequential Picture Cards (127)*[8] (another example of extended usage). After the tape has been played, scatter the picture cards on a desk and ask the child to put them in the correct order to match the story on the recorder. Then play the tape once more to see if it matches the pictures as the child arranged them.

8. Pick the word that does not belong in each group:

"Cat, fat, book, hat."

"Run, fun, sun, dig."

"Pencil, apple, orange, banana."

"Lion, house, tiger, monkey."

Children must remember all four words while thinking about the relationship between them, to decide on the correct answer.

9. Youngsters usually enjoy "thinking games." While these might be categorized under *auditory imagery,* they can also fit under auditory memory because the student must be able to retain all the clues to arrive at the solution. Teacher gives clues such as: "I'm thinking of something that runs on four legs and barks." Gradually increase the challenge such as, "I'm thinking of something that comes out of an oven and rhymes with 'lake,' or . . . something that begins like 'store' and is the opposite of 'go'."

With regular use of the techniques described above, we have had positive results. Most of the children who had been identified by their teachers as having short attention spans were able to concentrate for longer periods of time, absorb information presented orally, and remember much of it after a few months of working to develop those skills.

[7] *See* Sources.

[8] *See* Sources.

We must always be aware that each child is different and has a particular style of learning. By following our pragmatic philosophy ("If this method doesn't work, let's try the next"), we never give up on a child. At the very least, we feel we are helping the child build needed skills. At the very best, all the skills mesh to form a sound foundation upon which to base future cognitive development.

CHAPTER 8

Supplemental and Remedial Programs

Once the child's basic perceptual skills have been developed, we need to re-examine the original problems. What was he having trouble with in the classroom? Math? Reading? Spelling? Writing? Each subject that was causing the child distress needs to be retaught in a different way now.

Let's look at the student who found his way into the Child Development Program because he just couldn't seem to remember number facts, and consequently could not pass the timed drill tests conducted in his classroom. We've checked his visual and auditory memory skills and enhanced them using the techniques described in Chapters 6 and 7. Now we can present mathematics to him in a way that he will truly understand. When you really comprehend a concept, you're much more inclined to remember it.

Structural Arithmetic,[1] described in Chapter 3, was designed to be used with grades K–3 to give a kinesthetic and logical approach to learning arithmetic. It has proven to be helpful for older children who have not internalized mathematics using the more traditional programs which usually have stronger emphasis on rote learning. For several of our students, who were already in grades four and five when referred to the Child Development Program, *Structural Arithmetic* was truly a life-saver, turning these children around from failure to success. In the privacy of the Child Development room, we went back to the beginning level of experimentation with the blocks and rods and got rid of all the doubts and insecurities which had plagued these students for years. Beginning with the experimentation, manipulating the blocks and rods, as prescribed in the Teacher's Guide, we worked our way through the three levels of the program. While we did accelerate a bit to sustain the students' interest, we did not overlook any aspect of the information provided. Upon completion, the students were ready and able to do math at their grade level with true understanding and confidence.

If more schools were to place this math program into their primary curriculum there would be no need for a remedial approach to this subject. Start with the Introductory Guide and Set A to help children who have not yet learned what numbers really are, and consequently can't remember the number facts or when to use addition or subtraction.

Some students who can remember math facts, but have trouble with reading, experience difficulty with "story problems." They have to work so hard to decode words that they often guess at which operation is needed to solve a problem. It's clear that they need remedial reading or perhaps some other kind of help* for their difficulty. If they have a command of

---

[1] *Structural Arithmetic:* Originally published more than twenty years ago, and out-of-print for many years, it has recently been re-issued. *See* Sources.

*See Note, p. 131.

math facts, we can offer some help with a program called *How to Solve Story Problems*.[2] We have had positive experiences with this set of sequentially organized cards that provide students with the key words or phrases needed to determine which operation to use. The authors have expanded on this obviously well-received kit and now offer a group of six different ones. They are re-usable, sturdy cards with acetate covers and work well for individuals as well as small groups.

One very helpful hint that can make a big difference in the understanding of numbers, especially for children with perceptual problems is: *use graph paper*. When working with concepts of place value, the boxes keep the numerals neatly in the correct columns, making it easier to work even multiplication and long division problems. Working with decimals, keeping tenths, hundredths, etc. in their correct columns becomes so much easier. Graph paper, also called "quadrille," is available in different size squares. We use the 1-inch squares for our kindergarteners and first-graders, and the 1/2-inch for grades two, three, and four. Our fifth- and sixth-graders prefer the 1/4-inch squares. The Child Development Program has been using graph paper for math for years; it seems like such an obviously useful tool, yet it comes as a revelation to those who never thought of it. Another idea to share: if there is no graph paper available, use regular lined paper, turned sideways, so the lines run vertically. While not as desirable as graph paper, this is an improvement over the plain unlined paper that children are usually supplied with for computational work in most schools.

In today's schools, there are two key phrases gaining in popularity with regard to reading programs: "whole language" and "literature-based." There are good things to be said about all reading programs. The average child will learn to read with almost any instruction; in fact, some learn to read with no formal instruction, just by being read to by their parents. One note of caution to offer the young teachers in today's elementary classrooms: *don't forget about phonics*. In every kindergarten, first, and second grade classroom there are at least a few children who are not visual learners.*

These are the youngsters who can remember the stories read to them almost verbatim, and they love to hear the same ones again and again. But if you put some of those words into a different story and ask them to read it to you, they will have a very difficult time. If the classroom teacher does not allocate enough time for teaching phonics, these students are candidates for the Child Development Program. Here they will be offered the help they need through any one of several excellent supplemental programs for teaching children to read, write, and spell.

1. As an introduction to phonics in kindergarten or a developmental first grade, our first choice is the *Intersensory Reading Method*. With a box of small, familiar objects, we have a unique "hands-on" approach to teaching children to read. Already discussed in the early pages of Chapter 3, we repeat mention of it here because it can be used as a supplemental and/or remedial program.

2. One of the first "getting ready to read" programs we used was *Structural Reading*. By the same authors as *Structural Arithmetic*, it presents a systematic, logical approach to learning to read. Recently revised, it is probably better than ever.

[2] *See* Sources.
*See Note, p. 131.

3. *Primary Phonics*[3] and *More Primary Phonics* is a program that can be the first workbook to follow the "object box" experience. The skills developed through using the workbooks are practiced by the student in reading the little storybooks that are synchronized to be used at specific intervals. More than ten years of successful experience with this program leads me to endorse it warmly. The children love reading when it is made so easy for them.

4. *Get Ready for The Code,*[4] *Get Set for The Code,* and *Go for The Code.* These primers employ tracing, matching, tracking, copying, and following directions in attractive formats to help children learn which sounds go with which letters. Perfect for K and grade one, they precede the *Explode The Code* series.

5. Another worthwhile purchase is *Cove Reading with Phonics Program.*[5] Newly updated, this program is an outgrowth of extensive classroom teaching experiences with immature children and children with learning disabilities. It has helped our kindergarteners and slower first graders who needed extra practice to overcome the sound/symbol hurdle. The clear, uncluttered format makes it especially beneficial for students with short attention span and high distractibility. We suggest starting your order with *Getting Ready for Phonics, Parts I and II,* followed by *Consonants* and *Short Vowels* Workbooks.

6. The *Johnson Handwriting Program*[6] described in detail in Chapter 5 has helped so many children learn to write legibly that it deserves another mention here, along with *Beginning Connected Cursive Writing,*[7] which provides positive reinforcement for children after they have completed the first introductory pages on the Cursive Writing Forms included in this book.

Although some of the preceding programs duplicate services, variety is after all the spice of life. When you have used a program for a few years, achieving good results from it with the children, you almost hesitate to try anything new. On the other hand, if you don't try that new program, you'll never know how much more successful or more fun it might be. Rest assured that the above recommendations are based on years of positive experiences.

NOTE: We need to explore the possiblity that these children may need the services of a developmental optometrist. 20/20 sight in each eye does not guarantee that the eyes are working well together. While these children may learn *how* to read, the actual act of reading, i.e., focusing on a group of symbols, extracting meaning from this group of symbols, then moving on to the next group while still trying to retain the thought started by the preceding group might require more effort than they can put forth due to malfunctioning of the "teaming" mechanisms in the eyes. Think of the eyes as two horses hitched to a wagon. If one horse is aiming for the middle of the road while the other is aiming for the curb, the wagon driver will have some trouble moving forward smoothly. Likewise, if one eye is aiming at the first letter of a word while the other eye is aiming at the fourth letter in the same word, the

[3] *See* Sources.

[4] *See* Sources.

[5] *See* Sources.

[6] *See* Sources.

[7] *See* Sources.

child has difficulty decoding and comprehending what the word means, let alone remembering it while he has to attack the next word in this confusing manner. Most children with this problem are not aware of what is happening. Some of them discover that when they cover one eye, reading get easier for them, but it takes so much effort that they tend to avoid prolonged reading tasks. Homework that should take a half-hour drags on for three times that, and gets finished only through the perseverance of caring and determined parents. The child with this "hidden" problem may never develop to his fullest potential, because it permeates all of his activities, in the classroom, on the playing field, and at home.

The truth is that this condition is correctable through optometric vision training. Unfortunately, very few school systems are aware of the problem or the solution. In fact, many eye practitioners are unschooled in identifying or remediating the problem. See page 14 for sources of referrals to accredited developmental optometrists. Furthermore, it should be made clear to parents that if this problem does exist, children do not outgrow it any faster than they outgrow the need for orthodontia. If a child needs orthodontic appliances, does the school pay for them? Of course not. Following this line of reasoning, schools should not be expected to pay for vision therapy. It is the parents' responsibility.

CHAPTER 9

Administering the Child Development Program

The administration of any educational program requires planning, budgeting, and accountability. Salaries are paid by boards of education (taxpayers) with the hope of seeing positive results. In general, these results are measured by tests given to the students, or by the numbers of students that graduate each year, or the number of students that are accepted into colleges. One more number that school boards are watching is the cost of special education. Many school districts nationwide are experiencing escalating costs in this area as the classroom teachers refer more children to special services personnel for evaluation, which frequently results in classification and special class placement. Once the Child Development Program is established in your school district, you should expect to see a decline in referrals to special services. No doubt there will still be a few, but the large numbers of those with mild perceptual problems will be referred instead to the Child Development teacher.

When the originator of the Child Development Program left the North Brunswick Township school system, the leadership of the Program was passed on to the next school psychologist, and then to the director of Special Services. Each building principal also shared in its supervision, being responsible for observing and evaluating the Child Development teacher's work on a regular basis. Each year we submitted to both a report covering the accomplishments of the Child Development Program in our school, including the names, grades, and status of each child with whom we worked (C = Continue, D = Dismissed, M = Moved, R = Referred to Special Services). When requested, a statistical summary is completed: number of students enrolled, number of parent conferences, number of teacher conferences, etc.

The budget for new equipment and supplies has come from the Special Services account, supplemented if necessary by the building principal's account. Once the initial supply of non-consumable items described throughout these chapters has been acquired, we really don't need more than about $500 per year for consumable materials to service a student population of approximately 500 per building.

With regard to space requirements, the Child Development Program in John Adams School has always been in a small room, large enough to accommodate at maximum eight students at one time. Ideally, we try to establish groups of three or four, but occasionally must have a one-to-one time for certain students. The room needs to be large enough to use a balance beam and a rocking board. We need space between the desks to practice bouncing, jumping rope and skipping, although we have used the hallway for these activities at times, with no one suffering because of it. A place to hang the Marsden ball so that it can swing in a 36″ diameter circle, as well as space to hit it with a rolling pin-bat is a definite requirement. A large chalkboard should be attached to a wall low enough for five- and six-year-olds to do their chalkboard exercises. A magnetic board is a nice extra, but not a necessity. One or two filing cabinets, a large bulletin board and adequate shelf space round out the list of basic needs.

Maintaining a file of information about each participant is crucial for accountability. A folder in the "current" files would include the child's initial referral form filled out by the classroom teacher, principal or parent, all test results, notes of meetings held regarding the student, plus a copy of each report written about the child's performance in the Child Development Program, and his current work. Any printing, writing, or art work of which we are especially proud is mounted on display panels in the hallway just outside our room or on our bulletin board. Most of the children's work is sent home at the end of each marking period, after we have reviewed it with the parents.

Each year, a large daily plan book has been used to record an abbreviated list of every group's daily activities, along with materials used. This information was entered shortly after each session was completed. For an overview of what a child has done in the Child Development Program, the record can be read from the beginning to the end of his enrollment. His file folder is moved out of "current" records when he has completed his participation in the Child Development Program, but is maintained in a separate area until the child has moved on to other schools.

When deciding on a plan of action to help a child who is experiencing difficulties in his classroom, it's been a successful practice to use the child's strengths to build up his weaknesses. For example, when testing a child, if the auditory skills are weak but the visual skills are strong, try to use visual and motor clues to ensure his success while you work to develop the auditory areas. Let the classroom teacher know the results of your testing as soon as possible, along with practical suggestions which can be used to help the child become more successful. When the teacher feels that the Child Development Program is reaching out to help her as well as the child, everyone benefits. Try to enlist the involvement of the parents by letting them know the results of diagnostic tests promptly, along with specific recommendations which will benefit their child and strengthen the relationship between them.

These procedure guidelines have worked well in handling most cases:

1. Classroom teacher discusses child's problem with the principal and parents.

2. Classroom teacher discusses problem with Child Development teacher.

3. Child Development teacher observes child in classroom, then schedules diagnostic testing.

4. Child Development teacher checks records in office for prior history, nurse's sight and hearing test results, previous year's report card, etc.

5. Child Development teacher administers diagnostic tests (currently: Test of Visual-Motor Skills, Test of Visual-Perceptual Skills, and Test of Auditory-Perceptual Skills). Depending on the age and attention span of the child, the testing may take several sessions to complete.

6. Child Development teacher reviews results of tests with classroom teacher, principal, and parents (can be done on the phone if necessary, but better in person, with all present).

7. Child Development teacher consults with classroom teacher to set schedule for child's participation in Child Development Program, avoiding conflicts with instruction time and "specials" (art, music, phys. ed., computer) if possible.

8. Principal and parents are informed when child is scheduled to begin participation in Child Development Program.

9. Regular reports are made in the following manner:
   a. Narrative reports at the close of each marking period, one copy for parents, one copy for cumulative file in office, plus a copy in Child Development file.
   b. In-school conferences are held twice yearly (November and April) with classroom teacher and parents (on phone if necessary).
   c. Additional informal meetings between classroom teacher and Child Development teacher are vital for the child's success. As he begins to work in the Program, some progress should be apparent in his classroom within the first few weeks. Since success in the classroom is the ultimate goal, feedback from the classroom teacher is important for planning the child's daily work with the Child Development teacher. Aim for at least one five-minute meeting per week per child.
   d. Final reports in June should be written with recommendations for specific activities to be done during the summer.
10. Child Development teacher follows up with child's new teacher in September.

It is helpful and advisable for all the Child Development teachers in a school district to meet at least *once a month,* and more often if possible, during the first year to review cases and help each other with solutions that have worked. It is important to start at a level low enough so that the child feels able to accomplish what is asked. Show him *how* to do what you are asking of him. Stay at his side and be supportive and encouraging. Some children will need only a few weeks, others will need months. A few may need more than one year.

As spring approaches, the classroom teachers will need to prepare their lists of possible retentions. Some Child Development participants can move on to the next grade and still benefit from continued inclusion in the Program. Others may need to remain at their current grade level and develop more maturity and mastery of the situation. Still others may need the complete evaluation available from the Child Study team to determine the best academic placement.

It is important to hold district-wide meetings to inform the whole staff of the workings of the Child Development Program, what its purposes are and how helpful it can be to them. They should be pleased to see the Child Development Program established in their midst, and should not feel threatened by it. The Child Development Program should be viewed as a benefit to the teachers as well as the students. The Child Development teachers should think of themselves as partners with every teacher in the building. They have the same general duties as all the other teachers in the school, plus the role of liaison between the school and Special Services.

Near the end of each school year, as mentioned earlier, we have written a report highlighting the activities of the year—the things that were great as well as the ones that fell short of expectations. Whoever is administering the Child Development Program should read these and comment on them. In this way, the Program can be improved and each Child Development teacher can be assured that there is active communication at hand, and he or she is not operating in isolation.

Each participant's teacher should be consulted often to determine the extent of the carryover to the classroom of whatever has been done in the Child Development room. While we are attempting to affect positive change in the children that will help them for the rest of their lives, we are trying to assist them in their immediate situation, to become more successful students in their classrooms and happier more confident members of their peer groups. For these reasons, we need to have steady feedback from the classroom teachers, and keep them informed of the techniques we are employing. If our first plan of action is not bringing about the changes we are looking for, we must be ready to try another plan, and be ready to take suggestions from others, as well.

Anything new and different may be a little frightening at first. Those who are selected to be the Child Development teachers in your district should have at least three years of primary classroom experience first. Some graduate level courses in recognizing and working with learning disabilities would be helpful. These people must also be flexible, caring and warm, but self-assured and firm in dealing with children. They must have the capacity to inspire the children to perform. They need to set up the conditions for each child in the Child Development Program to be successful in at least one activity every day. The work must be made to appear as fun and "do-able." At the same time, it must be applicable to the ultimate goals that have been set for the child. In this age of accountability, one must be able to justify the use of whatever activities a child is being asked to do. "Busy work" has no place in the Child Development Program.

Once you let the children know that what they are doing in the Child Development Program will help them to do their regular school work better and more easily, chances are that you will get their cooperation. They should be made to feel very important and privileged to be allowed to work in this Program. It's not for just anybody; it's only for certain people who are capable of doing much better work than they have been doing, and want to learn how. Make it clear from the beginning that everyone in the Child Development Program has average or above average intelligence, and the potential to become whatever they set themselves as a goal. Then help them to achieve success. Little rewards, stickers, points to accumulate and trade in for special treats are part of the plan. The rewards reaped by the students in this Program are surpassed only by the gratifications derived by the Child Development teachers who see these underachievers go on to blossom and excel.

The Parent-Teachers Association should schedule at least one meeting a year featuring the Child Development Program to let parents become familiar with its purpose. Perhaps the Child Development teacher could also write a short column in the school newsletter about issues related to child growth and development.

An article in your local newspaper, once you have implemented the Child Development Program, is an excellent way to reach out to the community and let them know what a progressive educational system they have.

As for evaluation of the Child Development Program, the following three aspects are to be considered:

1. Facility of the Child Development teacher in developing rapport with individual children and teachers;
2. The mastery and presentation of the varied techniques along with the appropriateness of these procedures for the conditions of the child or children involved;
3. The results in terms of the improvement of the child in the measurable areas of perceptual-motor functioning and in the often unmeasurable areas of self-worth and attitudes about school and one's own success.

As Jay Roth concluded his report to the administration:

> It is essential to understand that children are not machines and that their feelings about their own competence directly affects their competence in a profound way. If a machine does not handle a problem correctly that difficulty can be corrected with a program modification; but simply modifying the program of a child is not enough, since that failure has affected much more than the program and his own sense of self must be a primary consideration. When a child is failing, it is therefore not enough to alter the environment; the child must be altered, for he has built within himself a feeling of failure which transcends the program. The child must be approached as a human being, and this, the Child Development Program attempts to do [1, p. 6].

REFERENCE

1. J. Roth, *Report to North Brunswick Township Board of Education,* March 21, 1969.

CHAPTER 10

Case Histories

Each year since September, 1968, fifty to sixty students have been enrolled in the Child Development Program at John Adams School for specific interventions, excluding the kindergarten classes with whom we work on a more preventive, developmental series of exercises.

These children were identified primarily by their classroom teachers who noted the symptoms of various learning problems on the initial referral forms. They came from every grade level in the school, and their difficulties ranged from being "unable to complete work independently" to "needs help in printing neatly." "Laurie sits through the explanation of all the independent work and as soon as I've finished she says 'What should I do?' Can you teach her to listen?" We had wheel-chair bound youngsters with spina bifida and paralysis from polio who learned to print and write legibly and read beautifully. At the other extreme, we had fast runners who won in the annual field day races, but had to learn to slow down their eye movements while copying from the board so they wouldn't skip words or lines. Most of our pupils were of average or above-average intelligence, and looked like ordinary children. They were recognized and referred to the Child Development Program because of their inability to do what their classmates were doing with ease. While some of our participants eventually were evaluated by the Child Study Team, classified and placed in special education classes, the overwhelming majority of our pupils developed the skills which had been lagging and went on to graduate with their peers.

Hitaishi, at the end of third grade was "Having trouble with cursive writing." A first-grade teacher reported about Mary Beth, "Eyes skip about the page in reading. Words are skipped, workbook activities missed as she skips about the page." Lisa's kindergarten teacher described her behavior: "Very quiet . . . doesn't recognize numerals or know value . . . doesn't recognize letters or hear sounds . . . frequent reversals of letters . . . just doesn't seem to understand what to do after having very detailed direction." (This case pre-dated our pre-K screening.)

Each child was different, yet we usually managed to group three or four for the services they needed. Some worked in the Child Development Program for a relatively short time (3 weeks for the almost-fourth grader to re-learn his cursive writing), while a few needed more than three years. The average term of enrollment was about six months. Each child was tested diagnostically and then re-tested periodically to determine what progress had been made following various interventive procedures.

It is difficult to pick just one case about which to write, so I have selected several, trying to give the reader a taste of what the Child Development Program does and how this affects those enrolled.

We'll start with Lisa described above who was referred at the end of February by her teacher after already being enrolled in speech therapy class. At the age of five years eight months, Lisa's auditory discrimination as measured by the Wepman test was grossly inadequate, with twenty errors out of forty trials. Her response on the Monroe auditory memory subtest was poor (5 items recalled of a possible 22), and her ability to repeat numbers heard was limited to three in a sequence. (It should be noted that this case from my files pre-dates the current perceptual tests we use which are more sophisticated, but we worked with what we had at the time.)

While Lisa could hop on each foot, skip, catch and throw a ball, bounce and catch a ball, and hit one on a string, the development of her fine motor coordination was lagging. Lisa had never been in pre-school or nursery school. Her speech was almost unintelligible. Her performance on the Gesell Copy Forms showed an ability to reproduce only the circle and cross successfully. Her "Draw-A-Person," while including the general configuration of the "little girl," was an unsmiling creature whose hands were attached to the upper trunk and was missing the ears and nose.

Following conferences with the classroom teacher, speech teacher, principal, and parents, Lisa was enrolled in the Child Development Program. Since she was in the morning kindergarten, we scheduled her to return to school for a half-hour every afternoon. She lived only a couple of blocks away, so this was acceptable to the parents.

Lisa joined a group of three kindergarten children reviewing following directions with chalkboard exercises from *Developing Learning Readiness,* parquetry blocks and eye movement training. We used the tape recorder with the "Polly Parrot" game, saying colors, letters, and numbers. The tachistoscope flashed numerals and letters to stimulate rapid recognition. We reviewed names of shapes and used templates to reproduce them, first at the chalkboard, then at the desks. Working on concepts of same and different, we used flannel board figures, blocks, and dittos with geometric designs. Within a few weeks, the children could identify the one digit out of four that was different in a tachistoscopic flash of less than one second. They could differentiate "right" and "left," and name the numbers to ten. We recorded sessions saying words that began like "boy" and "bat." Next, we played the tapes back and the children watched while I printed their words on the board. Each half-hour session gave us time to do at least two or three procedures.

By June her report stated: "Lisa has begun to show improvement in several areas . . . auditory sequencing, visual discrimination, and visual sequencing is better. Her general attitude is more positive and in great measure, she appears more alert to things around her." After conferences with parents, teachers (class and speech), and principal, it was agreed that Lisa would be best served by continuing her placement in kindergarten. She moved to the afternoon session, and was scheduled for Child Development in the morning with two other kindergarteners. They worked on fine motor, auditory and visual skills, all the while becoming more successful and confident.

By March, Lisa was printing the lower case letters correctly and tape recording words beginning with the letters used in the printing lesson each day. She could recognize numbers to 20 and make sets to correspond. After hearing a story with the *Sequential Picture Cards* on Thursday, Lisa could tell the same story and set up the cards appropriately on Friday. Progressing steadily, we worked on eye movements with the Marsden ball, as well as "green crayon (left fist)" — "red crayon (right fist)" — "teacher (front of room)." Using the tachistoscope, the children worked at identifying three numbers at a glance. We made "follow the dot" pictures, practiced bouncing to ten, and played dominoes—making numbers useful and part of their everyday world. We listened to records and followed the directions of the narrator, telling us which hand to wave and which foot to tap. We matched magnetic numbers to cards with sets of objects. A favorite game was feeling glass-beaded letters on small cards without looking at them, then going to the chalkboard to print them. We recorded rhyming words and did visual-memory dittos with shapes and numbers (which shape came first, which second)?

By May of her second year in kindergarten, Lisa was quite competent in printing the numerals to ten on the chalkboard as well as on paper. She could cut apart scenes from a story and paste them in the correct sequence. She could follow directions well. She had become more conversational in the group. All of her skills were developing, along with her confidence.

First grade brought a new teacher into Lisa's life who described her at the end of September as "a very shy child who needs a great deal of reinforcement and opportunities to express herself. New materials and concepts introduced to Lisa require repetition." Lisa continued with the Child Development Program. Building on the activities she had mastered, we went on to 4- and 5-digit recall, picking words that begin with the same sound, and more detailed oral directions to follow.

In November, we dropped Lisa's attendance to three times weekly; she was getting speech therapy twice a week and we didn't want her to miss too much class time. While we emphasized the auditory skills development, we continued with the visual and motor, integrating the three as often as possible. We clapped to the beat of a metronome, then walked on the balance beam to the same beat. Once again we reviewed the letters and the sounds they make.

Finally, in January of her first-grade year, Lisa seemed to be meeting with success and building her confidence in the classroom. Re-testing the skills which had been weak in June, we found improvement in every area. Auditory discrimination on the Wepman showed impressive progress (only 2 errors in 40 trials). Lisa's visual-motor and visual-memory skills had developed: her printing was neat and well-placed. I suggested a temporary "leave" from the Child Development Program at the end of January, noting that she would continue in the speech program and assuring her teacher that I would take Lisa back if she showed any regression.

In September, her second-grade teacher referred Lisa to the Reading Specialist who, after testing her, suggested that Lisa's needs in reading were more developmental than remedial, and requested that she return to the Child Development Program. On the referral form, her classroom teacher noted Lisa's speech difficulties and continued, "A possible slow learner. Very cheerful, helpful, interested. Tries hard—is gaining more confidence with extra classroom help. Loves school—very tuned in."

Lisa, who had twice been described as "very quiet" and "shy" became a leader in the small Child Development group. Using the *Intersensory Reading Method* to review the language arts skills, she participated enthusiastically. Once this was completed, we expanded her learning by writing our own little stories, playing word games such as *Anagrams* and composing word problems to practice other academic skills such as addition and subtraction.

We advised regular practice in both language arts and math during the summer following grade two, to prevent loss of those skills, and that was the last time that Lisa needed the Child Development Program.

It should be noted that the year Lisa was in second grade, we instituted the pre-kindergarten screening which is still done each May. If we had found Lisa before she entered kindergarten, we could have helped her earlier, and perhaps her progress could have been accelerated. As it happened, Lisa's younger sister was enrolled in the John Adams School speech program *and* a local nursery school on my recommendation at the first meeting with Lisa's parents. Laura came to kindergarten far better prepared than Lisa had been.

Speaking with Lisa's mother recently, I was told that Lisa had graduated from the county vocational-technical school, becoming a baker at a local bakery and had enjoyed the work very much. Now Lisa is married and a full-time mother of twins.

*   *   *   *

Hitaishi was nearing the end of third grade when he entered our school. He had missed all of the formal class instruction in cursive writing, and his teacher presented me with a sample of his work which was very hard to read. Could anything be done for this child before he reached fourth grade? Hitaishi was very willing to learn and was goal-directed. Following the Johnson handwriting method described in Chapter 5, using the cursive writing paper with slanted lines, we did four letters per day, top half of each page in class, immediately after the chalkboard introduction to each letter. Hitaishi would then take the page home and repeat the tracing and practice of each letter that evening. In this manner, he learned the correct formation and placement of all the letters, lower case and capitals in the final three weeks of school that year.

*   *   *   *

Mary Beth had entered our school in first grade, thus missing out on our developmental training in kindergarten. She was referred to the Child Development Program on October 6th, and tested on October 7th and 14th, when she was five years ten months old. She was very quick in her movements, taking just fifty-two seconds to do the visual discrimination test we used at the time, in which she scored only four correct of ten trials. Her responses on the Gesell Copy Forms showed disorganization, and poor reproduction of all shapes except the circle and cross. She had difficulty bouncing a ball, but the real problem, as her perceptive classroom teacher had indicated, was in Mary Beth's erratic eye movements.

Within two weeks after the referral, testing was completed and conferences were held with the teacher, principal, and parents. Mary Beth started in the Child Development Program on October 25th, using Heinsen's *Visual Motor Development* exercises, the *Ann Arbor Symbol Tracking* book, and some of the saccadic exercises described in Chapter 6. We worked on correct formation and placement of letters using the *Look and Write* program. We used the sensory-system matching pages ("Oink, quack, etc.") to train Mary Beth and the others in her group to follow across a line of print from left to right smoothly, and then continue to the next line. They continued in this manner with the steady tapping of the metronome set at sixty beats per minute.

The children took turns lying on the rug mats beneath the Marsden ball, developing smooth visual tracking as the ball swung clockwise and counterclockwise, as well as horizontally, vertically, and diagonally above them. While one was busy with this exercise, the others would be practicing "rainbow tracing" (following a dotted pattern with each color crayon), or working with a large rubber ball on "drop-and-catch" in another corner of our little Child Development room.

By January, Mary Beth was finding the letters in alphabetical order in the *Ann Arbor Letter Tracking* book. We continued with the saccadic exercises from both Heinsen's and Getman's programs. Using the tachistoscope, we worked to grasp three and then four letters at a glance, and write them down. Mary Beth was doing this successfully by the end of January. Her visual pursuits were now smooth and sure. She was ready to leave the Child Development Program. From October 25th to February 8th, we had changed the way she functioned. Her final report noted "considerable progress in the development of eye-hand coordination and smooth eye movements." No longer was she omitting words or skipping lines as she read. Her printing was clear and properly placed.

On the final report is a space for recommendations; it read, "Maintain watchfulness—if there is any return of problematic visual/motor functioning, notify Child Development immediately. Parents plan to have Mary Beth's eyes checked by family eye doctor; follow recommendations which may result."

Two years later, Mary Beth returned to the Child Development Program for work in cursive writing. This involved attendance three times weekly for the final fifteen minutes of the day. Our Handwriting Clinic gave her and six other fourth- and fifth-graders an opportunity to review the correct formation and placement of the letters, after which they used their improved writing to practice their weekly spelling words.

* * * *

While doing the research for these case histories, I glimpsed the names of many children with whom I worked. I wonder how they fared through the rest of their schooling. It would be unrealistic to imagine that every one of them went on to be 100 percent successful in everything. What I hope to hear when I'm lucky enough to reach the parents is that their child completed school and became a productive member of society.

Occasionally I meet a former student. Once he or she recovers from the shock of having been recognized, we chat for a few minutes about what has transpired in the process of growing up. I was pleased when one young man who was delivering a floral arrangement from his shop commented, "You were the teacher who taught me how to learn!" A young woman with whom I worked when she was in fifth grade and needed a complete review of math with the *Structural Arithmetic* program is now a college graduate, successfully working with computer programming.

* * * *

One of the most gratifying experiences of my career has been with Terry McCarthy. He was referred by his kindergarten teacher at the end of September (before we instituted our pre-K screening) with the following problems: "Poor motor coordination—poor grasp of crayon—has no idea how to color—when given assistance he doesn't tune in—too interested in what other children are doing. Wears glasses . . . speech problem also." He was five years two months old.

Terry's speech and sight problems were being addressed by other professionals, and since the teacher had specifically requested help with his motor coordination, that became my target. At that time, Terry could not skip or bounce a ball. He hopped and jumped with great difficulty. His Gesell Copy Forms were piled on top of each other, showing how weak his organizational skills were, and his formation of the shapes was very immature. He scored 17/30 – 1/10 on the Wepman Auditory Discrimination Test, indicating very inadequate development of that skill. In auditory memory, however, he scored age-appropriately and his ability to repeat sequences of numbers verbally was excellent. Terry had great difficulty maintaining visual attention.

Realizing Terry's severe developmental lags in all motor skills, we started on a large mat on the floor, with basic beginning forms of movement: rolling, hopping like a jack rabbit (first the arms, then the legs), then moving like a crocodile, (on his belly, arms, and legs). We sat on the floor and rolled a large playground ball back and forth, practicing aiming and catching. We used all the gross motor programs of Getman and Heinsen, incorporating Terry's strength in auditory memory and sequencing to build his sense of rhythm.

The Buzzer Board helped Terry to walk on the divided balance beam; verbal input along with red bracelets on his right hand and foot heightened his awareness of directionality. The large red X targets used in the mat and balance beam exercises helped Terry develop his visual fixation skills. We used the tachistoscope to build Terry's ability to recognize all the shapes. Next, by tracing them first on the chalkboard with templates, then on the desk with acetate covers, his own geometric shapes became recognizable. We progressed to dot-to-dot and cut-and-paste pictures. Using the *Stepping Stones* described in Chapter 6, Terry started his alternate hopping which would become skipping.

By the end of December, all five kindergarteners in the group were succeeding in tossing and catching a playground ball, recognizing, matching, and drawing the basic shapes and forming them in clay. We did a lot of reviewing, and introduced a new exercise every few days, thus building skills while keeping interest high. Interspersing fine and gross motor activities, we used bead stringing and parquetry blocks, developing patterns of colors and shapes while building manipulative dexterity. We practiced printing names, cutting straight lines, reproducing designs on peg boards, drawing self-portraits, pinching clothespins, and squeezing chunks of clay. Terry practiced tossing bean bags into baskets, hitting the Marsden ball with the "rolling pin bat," watching it circle above as he lay on the mats below it, developing smooth eye movements. His attention span was growing while he learned to do parquetry puzzles and reinforced his visual sequencing with "What comes next?" tasks. By doing a minimum of three and maximum of five activities in each daily half-hour session, we gave Terry and his groupmates opportunities for successful reinforcement as well as creative challenge, keeping them happily plugging away toward their goals.

The June re-testing indicated that Terry was more successful in organizing and replicating the Gesell Copy Forms. His visual-motor-memory achievement showed that he could retain and reproduce what his eyes had learned to fixate upon, with a score on the Monroe #3 of 7/16, which was average for an almost-six-year-old.

Summer Child Development sessions during July reinforced what Terry had learned and extended his use of these skills. The tachistoscope helped him speed up visual recognition of shapes, numbers, and letters, which he then practiced forming on the chalkboard and paper. The tape recorder helped to develop and review auditory discrimination, which in turn helped his speech to become more articulate (teacher said 3 words; children picked the 2 that began with the "t" sound, etc.)

As he entered first grade, Terry could recognize all the letters and numbers but his motor skill development lagged; he still found it difficult to maintain his fixation on any target for longer than a couple of minutes. It's hard to catch a ball without looking at it, and it's hard to print when you aren't looking at the pencil and paper. A bright, agreeable child, Terry wanted to please all the adults in his life. He was trying and succeeding in tiny increments. We both had enormous patience and by making the work appear to be games, we made all this effort seem to be fun.

Terry's performance on the *Clymer-Barrett* test at the beginning of grade one was encouraging: in visual discrimination tasks, he missed only two items out of fifty-five. His self-portrait was much improved over the preceding year, but was missing the arms. His auditory skills measured in the adequate range, with some additional practice needed in matching ending sounds. Terry continued his participation in the Child Development Program with three other first grade boys, doing the exercises from Getman and Heinsen again, reviewing stepping stones again, learning how to tie a bow (pre-Velcro days), and, incredibly, not ever complaining.

On December 1st, the boys started to weave potholders on small metal looms. The fact that this was to be a Christmas gift for his mother made it very important to Terry and he really became "focused." The concepts of "over" and "under" took on new meaning as his manipulative skills were being sharpened. We did many other activities during the month, but when the boys finished their potholders on the 20th and we wrapped them in bright paper, the look of pride on their faces was extremely gratifying.

After almost daily practice on the wide variety of motor activities, January 10th of his first grade year, Terry skipped down the hall. Marsden ball and bat, eye movement exercises, left/right activities, chalkboard circles, lines, shapes, while maintaining fixation on the "X," using magnetic letters to form word "families," i.e., cat, hat, mat; ten, hen, men, etc., along with bounce-and-catch—all were beginning to pay off for him. On March 23rd, he learned to tie his shoelaces. Terry could use rubber bands on geoboards to copy patterns and was meeting success in completing designs on the visual-motor ditto sheets. When he walked the balance beam, he could now point with the opposite hand and count his steps at the same time. Reviewing concepts of top-left, bottom-right, etc. was the beginning of the *Look and Write* program, which helped Terry find the correct place to start each letter, along with the correct way to form it and place it on paper. By May, Terry managed to bounce and catch an 8″ playground ball twice without losing control of it. He had developed enough aiming power to play "Hit the Disk" [8, p. 86].

Following his second July in the Summer Child Development Program, his teacher reported, "Terry has shown slight improvement in his fine and gross motor control," and recommended that he continue working on these skills in second grade, to help "refine his printing." Amazingly, his enthusiasm remained high. Terry served as a leader in the activities as we reviewed all the bilateral arm and leg movements, chalkboard circles, lines, and walking to rhythm. Practice in printing included making the letters from clay and printing them on the chalkboard. Using anagram letters, Terry formed words to demonstrate the short and long vowel sounds, then copied them into a booklet, changing the capitals to lower case letters. If he could read his own printing several days later, he would earn an extra star. When he felt confident in his printing, he began taking dictation on these words.

Still brushing up on bouncing, cutting, and batting the Marsden ball, Terry's schedule was reduced to four sessions per week. He was good at catching the letters flashed by the tachistoscope, his printing was improving and he was becoming more proficient at other motor tasks such as weaving, and doing sewing cards while he and his groupmates played thinking games using rhyming words and clues. Starting each session with large muscle warm-ups, we then worked on a challenge such as, "How many words can you find in *imagination?*" which kept Terry and his group busily thinking and printing for fifteen minutes. Dominoes was a favorite visual discrimination and visual motor game which was used as a reward for prompt completion of a printing exercise. The *Ann Arbor Tracking* books were added to the list of activities which Terry practiced regularly: gross motor work on the floor mat, walking on the balance beam, rocking left and right, then forward and back on a rocking platform, doing the chalkboard circles all four ways, and the Marsden ball exercises. Toward the end of second grade, the group was taught checkers which promptly replaced dominoes as a "work quickly" bonus. By this time, the boys were composing, printing, and illustrating their own stories which we posted on the hall bulletin board.

Terry's improvement in all areas was becoming apparent and he was given the summer off, to just play and practice riding his two-wheeler. As he entered grade three, his participation in the Child Development Program was limited to the 8:45 to 9:00 A.M. slot before school really started each day. It gave us time for a smooth transition from manuscript to cursive writing, doing one letter a day plus the *Tracking* book, Marsden ball, and eye movement exercises. When the physical education teacher asked if we could work on "squat thrusts," we included that in our daily plan. "Thumb jumps" were added to the eye movement exercises, yarn ball catch, and the rocking platform exercise was now accompanied by clapping and counting. Along with practicing the capital letters in cursive, Terry was following the *Visual Motor Development* "awareness level creeping" and December 3rd, his chalkboard circles were done beautifully. This meant that he could control his eye movements and keep his fixation on the "X" during the bilateral production of ten circles on each side of the "X," using only his peripheral vision to guide his hands. (See Illustration 1, originally *Visual Motor Development* unit 5b.) The sensory-system matching ("Oink, quack . . .") and chalkboard star (Illustration 2, originally *Visual Motor Development* unit 5d) all helped. By then, Terry was able to catch five letters on the tachistoscope very successfully.

Nearing the end of grade three, Terry had developed legible handwriting, and rode his two-wheeler without the training wheels. He could do just about everything that his classmates could do. The reevaluations done at the end of each year showed the improvement that took place in his motor control. His self-portraits reflected the rise in his self-esteem. The samples of his printing and writing are testimony to the tremendous progress Terry made during the four years of work to overcome his severe developmental lag in motor coordination and control. The speech correction program under the guidance of Janet Kriner and Robert Connelly helped Terry considerably and made it possible for him to take leading roles in the class plays which were produced on the stage of a rather large auditorium.

Years later, when he was a college sophomore, Terry stopped by to say "Hello." He had decided, after much thought, that he wanted to help others the way he had been helped, and was studying to become an Occupational Therapist. He very graciously agreed to write about

chalkboard symmetry:
motor equivalence

purpose To develop a child's counter-balancing reflexes and equality of action between the two sides of the body.

equipment Chalk and chalkboard.

set up Ask the child to stand in front of a chalkboard, close enough that his nose touches the board. Have him mark an "x" at that point. The "x" becomes his eye level fixation point.

procedure 1 Ask the child to stand in front of the board in a relaxed chalkboard posture, holding a piece of chalk in each hand.

Figure 1

2 The child simultaneously draws two circles twelve to fifteen inches in diameter while fixating on the "x". The right circle is drawn counterclockwise and the left clockwise (Figure 1). Allow the child to compare the circles for similarity. He continues to practice, tracing over his own lines, striving to create figures that are both circular and equal in size.

Figure 2

3 The same as 2 except that now the left circle is drawn counterclockwise and the right circle clockwise. (Figure 2).

Illustration 1.

Figure 3

4   Both circles are clockwise (Figure 3).

Figure 4

5   Both circles are counterclockwise (Figure 4).

6   Repeat 2 through 5 with the circle about twelve inches above his eye level fixation point.

7   Repeat 2 through 5 with the circles above twelve inches below his eye level fixation point.

8   The child should practice **motor equivalence** for approximately five minutes per training session.

keys to improvement   The child is able to coordinate the movements of both hands simultaneously and effortlessly.

Illustration 1. (Cont'd.)

chalkboard symmetry: bimanual lines

purpose To develop the child's counter-balancing reflexes in space to such a degree that bilaterality of direction and side is implicit.

equipment Chalk and chalkboard.

set up

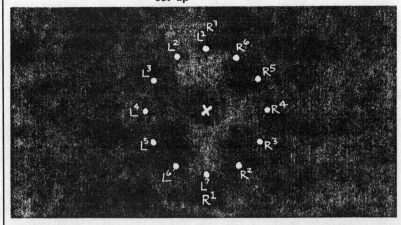

1 Establish the child's eye level fixation point as in **procedure b** of this unit.

2 Arrange a series of 12 dots around the fixation point, spread as on a clock, to form a circle about three feet in diameter. Label the dots as illustrated.

procedure

1 Fixating upon the "x" and holding chalk in each hand, the child places his chalk upon two directly opposite dots (e.g., L 4 and R 4) called out by you or a helper. He locates the dots through his peripheral vision.

2 The child draws a chalk line from the numbers to the central "x" and back to the numbers, repeating the motion with both hands simultaneously five times.

3 The above steps are repeated for other combinations of dots located in opposition to each other.

4 When the child begins to demonstrate proficiency, the activity should be carried out utilizing dots that are not in direct opposition (e.g., L 2 and R 3).

5 **Bimanual lines** should be practiced for about five minutes per training session.

keys to improvement

1 The hands move in unison.

2 The hands move in any direction freely.

3 The child places his chalk in the peripheral targets accurately.

4 The lines are straight and appear neat, one line over the other.

5 The activity is carried out smoothly, and with rhythm.

Illustration 2.

his experiences while a participant in the Child Development Program and his thoughts appear as Chapter 11 in this book.

Very few children have needed to work as hard developing their skills as Terry did. I don't want to think of what might have become of Terry had the Child Development Program not been there for him. His parents were warm, loving, and entirely supportive. They followed all the suggestions we made to help their son and we all took pride in Terry's accomplishments. He has graduated from college and is an Occupational Therapist.

CHAPTER 11

"My Experience with the Child Development Program"
by Terry McCarthy

One of my favorite television programs is "Wonder Years." The program is about a young boy in his preteen and teenage years growing up in the mid- and late-sixties and early seventies. The program doesn't talk about the death of JFK or Martin Luther King or the moon walk or Vietnam war protest in large theoretical terms or how they impact America's youth and their families. Instead the program tells stories about this boy and his friends and his family. What I enjoy about the program is that you obtain from it a true feeling of what it was like to be that age in that time. Probably more of a feeling for that time than you would have received from an historical program discussing the events of that era and the culture surrounding it very directly.

I thought about this program when I was asked to write this chapter about my experience with the Child Development Program as implemented in the John Adams Elementary School of North Brunswick, New Jersey. Like the viewer of "Wonder Years," I'd like the reader of this chapter to have a genuine feeling for what it is like to be a child with learning disabilities, and delayed fine and gross motor coordination. I will not list the difficulties I experienced by their technical names, or the ways they can be addressed by treatment of this type or therapy. I hope that by reading my story one can gain an appreciation for how a child feels when faced by these troubling and mysterious difficulties and how a child feels when he or she is empowered to overcome these difficulties, to achieve and create and learn and grow. At times this achievement and growth is stark and dramatic. At other times it is slow and halting, almost undetectable, but I am proof positive that through loving support and programs like Sue Levine's Child Development Program, it is possible.

I grew up much like the boy in "Wonder Years" and millions of other children in the late sixties and seventies in suburbia, in a development where every third house was the same as yours and there were fences between them. My street was not a through street, but a horseshoe, and we lived at the top of the curve. Behind my house and all the others on that side of the street was a large vacant field that in the years to come would fill up with warehouses and garden apartments, covering the pond where we used to skate every winter. Every sixth house had a basketball net and backboard on a pole, and that was the activity of choice in the spring. In the summer there were kids running through sprinklers in every front and back yard. In the fall there was talk of football and on Saturdays everyone was at the Rutgers game, where they played those perennial power houses: Princeton, Lehigh, and Colgate. In the winter there was actual tackle football played in the street shaped like a horseshoe that they never plowed.

I mention all this because it was the backdrop and I was a part of it and enjoyed all of it, but probably not as much as I should have, because I was different. The first manner in which I was different was my speech. I don't think it dawned on me at the time that my speech was impaired. I remember saying my name (Terry) once to adults. "Timmy?" came the response, and then, "Oh, Jerry?" Then, "Barry?" And then just quizzical looks. Now my name isn't that common, but I should have suspected something wasn't quite right with the way I was saying it. It wasn't until much later in life when I listened to my voice on tape from when I was five and wanted to be a "palma" (farmer), that I realized why at three and four only my mother could understand what I was saying.

I am proud of my speaking ability now. I did some theater in high school and college and my profession (occupational therapy) relies very much on my ability to verbally relay information to the parents, physicians, and caregivers of the children I treat. Yet the quality of my voice still bothers me. I can't stand hearing my voice on tape or videotape. Speech therapy, though simple, wasn't always easy, but it was easy to understand and work at. The therapy was fairly direct and narrowly focused which must have made it seem easier than it actually was. I had several therapists, but two wonderful people stand out in my mind: Mrs. Janet Kriner and Mr. Robert Connelly. They always rewarded my effort and made me feel like I was making progress toward something special.

In contrast to the speech work which was simple and direct, and which I felt was within my ability to do, the rest of school and growing up was not simple. I could not identify the problems so easily and listen to the rest of my life played back on tape. So without verbalizing them, my life at ages four, five, six, seven, and beyond became a series of at that time unanswerable questions. Following are the questions from my childhood. They could be any child's questions that can become doubts about themselves, that can replace knowledge and certainty about what one can accomplish.

Why am I always last in all of the swimming or running races, and don't throw a ball as far or as well as the rest? Why can't I serve a volleyball with one hand while throwing it up with the other, or hit a baseball with a bat even once? Why don't I like models, like all the other boys do? Why are they so hard for me that I just wind up throwing out half of my birthday presents because they were models? Why is it so hard for me to write neatly that I have to take my spelling test into a tape recorder and be different? Why do I always need to ask the teacher for more time when I am writing words down from the blackboard and be different? Why does it take me so long to write reports that I don't even want to start them? Why am I always picked last for the team and then the ball is never even passed to me?

Why do I always eat with my mouth open or drool when I am excited or concentrating? Why do I eat with my fingers or hold my fork wrong, even though my parents tell me not to? Why can't I stop gagging when I eat something lumpy, or feel something I don't like the feel of, like soap? The gagging and drooling are embarrassing; I should want to stop so why can't I? Why can't I go down or up the stairs with one foot on each step, alternating like everyone else? Why can't I hop up and down on the trampoline like the other kids, instead of the little bounces that are all I seemed able to do? Why did I find it so hard as a child to make friends and feel accepted by a group, even when I wanted to so badly? Why is it so hard for me to tie my shoes? Why do I put my coat or shirt on inside out or backwards? Why does Mom always need to remind me to brush my teeth or do the other stuff I need to do in the morning?

These are questions that build into doubts that come from my experience, but they could be the questions of thousands of school children. The exact answers or actual disabilities aren't as important as how we take the children from their questions and doubts and show them their real abilities and, yes, in some cases, disabilities. I do believe that we need to demonstrate that there are answers to these questions, and that the reasons for their difficulties are largely beyond their control. They are not at fault by not trying hard enough, not listening, or by being disobedient. In short, these questions directed to all of us require responses that affirm the child's effort and abilities.

What was difficult and frustrating to me as a child was having someone think that if he repeated directions over and over and over, it would improve my performance. It made me feel, since they kept repeating the same information in exactly the same way, that they thought either I wasn't listening or wasn't trying very hard. This happened to me in any number of situations and it is very easy as parents, educators, and therapists to slip into these nonproductive responses to a child's performance, especially when the child appears to be "in a rut." What was helpful for me, and what we must strive to do, I believe, is to respond in a way that directs the child's efforts into fun and achievable tasks that make the most of his or her abilities. These enjoyable and successful experiences work toward the desired objective: completing the tasks which were frustrating to the child in the first place.

Although I have spoken of the questions and frustrations I had as a child, I was blessed with many people in my life who were affirming of my talents and abilities in the manner described. My grandfather was not just an old man at a distance, but a wonderful friend, companion and buddy to whom, I remember, everything I did was positive. My parents were in the trenches with me every day, laboring to point out the gifts and abilities that I was blessed with, that made me special and unique. Even though they didn't know the exact answers to my questions, they probably had many similar questions of their own as to why their child had at times such intransient difficulties. I feel passionately that parents need their questions answered as clearly and concisely as possible, and when "We don't know," or "We're not sure" would be the truthful response, they need to be told that as well. My parents also responded with action: putting up balls with strings for me to hit with rolling pins, and building a low, square board that rocked for me to balance on, as was recommended by Sue Levine in her role as Coordinator of the Child Development Program. They will never be forgotten for the scores of unconsecrated eucharistic host which they had me practice swallowing without gagging every morning and night before my first holy communion in the Catholic Church.

Another major affirming force in my life was Sue Levine and her Child Development Program. It was there that I remember my first feeling of pride at accomplishing something with my hands and eyes together. I do not remember a task, whether it was weaving a potholder, drawing a picture, playing bounce and catch, or hitting a ball on a string with a rolling pin that ever left me feeling discouraged or overwhelmed. I don't remember exactly how she did it. But I suspect from my experience as a therapist that she did it by adapting the activity to make it successful and meaningful for me. In my four school years in the Child Development Program, including at least one summer session, all my questions were not answered. However, I was certain about what I was able to accomplish while I was there. Sue Levine's presence, warmth and loving encouragement were probably a large part of the feeling I obtained from the Program. She consistently made me feel that she had in some way gone out of her way to make sure the tasks I did with her were fun and that I was in some way able to do them. Therefore, I also felt I was special to her. I am sure a lot of her students felt the same way.

There were other reaffirming voices and experiences in those formative years: teachers, a few friends, and accomplishments. Another came from a usually distant source, my elementary school principal, Andrew Costello. I always felt, and have learned for a fact in recent years, that he went out of his way to look out for me. Not only for my educational needs, but for me, personally, to form a bond and, in short, to be a help. An example would be the time he took to be with me and put my makeup on before I starred in the school play "A Christmas Carol." I was Scrooge. I was in sixth grade, my last in John Adams School and in the audience were my parents, grandparents, and Sue Levine. At the end of the show, the first face I remember seeing was Mr. Costello beaming at me, as I received one of the warmest embraces I can recall.

This is my story and like any story it must have an ending. Yet my life is not over and my struggle with my questions will not be over until my life is. My fine motor coordination is not what it is for most people; ask anyone who has seen my typing. It takes me ninety minutes to write a medium-sized letter to a friend and an hour to write six or seven Christmas cards. I still struggle with which is my right and left at times. I will never be a guitarist, but I am the first to start a sing-along. I still forget my wallet and keys, but not an important birthday. I will never be an athlete, but I treasure my playtime with my cousin's children. I will never be a painter of beautiful pictures, but I take nice photos. I certainly will never be a mechanic, but I am a damn good cook.

If this particular story must end, it must, but I don't want it to because I have learned so much from writing it. In the end, let it be said that Terry did grow up. He grew up a bit more accepting of himself because of help received from Mrs. Levine, Mr. Costello, and his parents, all of whom seemed to be working together. He is able to give love and receive love from his friends and family. He works now as an Occupational Therapist with infants and children with delays, hoping their questions about their abilities don't become doubts about themselves. Every day, he works to make sure that most of what they do together is fun and that all is possible.

CHAPTER 12

History and Overview
of the Child Development Program

The Child Development Program of North Brunswick, New Jersey, was designed in 1967 as an immediate intervention, in an educational setting, to help children in grades one through six who were having difficulty meeting the requirements of their grade in school. It was conceived by a school psychologist, Dr. Jay Roth, who theorized that mild perceptual problems caused most learning difficulties. When children with these difficulties were allowed to continue unassisted, they would develop emotional insecurities caused by their frustration and poor self-esteem. They would give up trying to perform as directed and instead would either act out and disrupt classes, or drop out of school.

Dr. Roth's proposal, to place one teacher trained to remediate learning disabilities in each of North Brunswick's elementary schools, was initially supported by an E.S.E.A. Title I grant. When these funds were no longer available, the Board of Education, following the recommendation of then Superintendent of Schools, James Clancy, voted to include the Child Development Program as part of the school district's Special Services. The intention was to keep Child Study Team evaluations and classifications of students and their assignments to special education classes to a minimum. This proved to be a sound investment. Hundreds and possibly thousands of students over the past twenty-eight years would have required special education classes if they had not received the services of the Child Development Program in overcoming their developmental deficits, permitting them to remain and achieve success in the mainstream of education. This translates into millions of dollars saved for the taxpayers of North Brunswick. But this was only an extra added attraction. The main beneficiaries were those students who thrived from its services, as the Child Development Program saved lives, gave new hope and encouragement, helping many students to become productive and successful members of society.

From each of North Brunswick's elementary schools, one teacher was selected to be trained in the remediation of learning disabilities. The first participants were Neysa Bibel, Jean Bryson, Ann Marie Gorgas, and Martha Palmer. Along with Dr. Roth and Helene Benczik, who supervised North Brunswick's remedial reading program, they toured the state visiting many of the special educational facilities, evaluation clinics, and allied professionals. They read articles, books, and professional journals learning how to recognize and treat the various symptoms of learning difficulties. They prepared a curriculum, which continues to be updated as new materials and new ideas come on the market. Then they began to look at the children in their schools with enlightened vision. Speaking with the classroom teachers, they asked for those students who were having trouble meeting the demands of the grade.

At that time, the educational approach to learning disabilities was in its infancy. Special education served only three classifications: mentally retarded, emotionally disturbed/socially

155

maladjusted, and neurologically impaired. When a child was classified in any of these categories, education was usually provided in a special class or institution, not always available in the home district. The child who had only a mild perceptual problem was not usually recognized as such, and because he stared out the window instead of doing his classwork, was more apt to be thought of as an unmotivated daydreamer, and unfortunately, in the upper elementary grades became the class clown or troublemaker.

In September, 1968, the following tests were used by the Child Development teachers to profile the strengths and weaknesses of these underachievers:

Gesell Copy-Forms (visual motor)
Jan-Tausch (visual memory)
Ravens Matrices (visual perception)
CD Teachers (visual discrimination)
Wepman (auditory discrimination)
Monroe (auditory memory)

The information gathered was helpful in designing a plan for remediation which would then be implemented by the Child Development teacher. The classroom teachers now had a partner who could offer and provide help with that "problem" child, both in the classroom and in the Child Development room (usually a small room, but large enough to seat at least 6 students, with a window or skylight, chalkboard, proper lighting, and ventilation). There was flexibility built into the Program, permitting the child to leave his room for specific training that might interfere with classwork in progress. Consideration was shown in scheduling, to avoid having the child miss any new instruction while out of the classroom.

The first couple of years, most of the emphasis was on diagnosing and remediating learning problems and helping the classroom teachers to recognize the earliest signs and ask for intervention. With the publication of the Early Detection Inventory (a checklist of skills expected to have been developed in children at entrance age to kindergarten) and permission from then John Adams School principal Andrew Costello, we moved into the kindergartens at the beginning of September and started to identify youngsters who needed help, sometimes even before their teachers were aware that they had a problem.

Once identified, these pupils were assigned to work for twenty minutes daily with the Child Development teacher, when possible at a time other than their regular classtime. Since kindergarten was in session for only two-and-one-half hours daily, a morning student in need of developmental assistance could be back in school for a half-hour of Child Development work after lunch. The parents were very cooperative and excellent results were achieved in practically all cases of this early involvement to develop basic perceptual skills.

When some parents could not bring their kindergarteners back for this special assistance, the decision was made to give all kindergarten students at least six weeks (and more if necessary) of Developing Learning Readiness and "Perception +." This was done with the cooperation and participation of the kindergarten teachers. Scheduling these programs to take about fifteen minutes three times per week, they have been instrumental in developing gross and fine motor coordination, balance, smooth eye movements, form perception, visual discrimination, visual memory and spatial awareness as well as language and cognition. Although the original plan was to use these activities for the first six weeks, we have usually kept them going through December.

Most significant is the fact that children who experienced these developmental programs in kindergarten rarely needed remedial reading, remedial math, or resource room help in later years. Overwhelmingly, both the remedial reading and math programs have been populated by students who entered North Brunswick schools in first grade and beyond.

Continually looking for ways to improve the Program, in 1975 we pioneered the *pre*-kindergarten screening. With a kindergarten entrance birthdate in those days of December 31st, we were getting many enrollees who were not ready for school. The screening gave us the opportunity to collect considerable information about each child which was helpful to the kindergarten teachers, and to advise parents of any potential problems, some of which could be ameliorated with their help.

As new children moved into the school district, the Child Development teachers worked with the Reading Specialists to determine the best grade placements and whether the need for any remediation was indicated. If, for example, a fourth-grader moving in from Duncan, Oklahoma, in January had not yet been taught long division, but in North Brunswick, had already missed the first two units on long division, the Child Development teacher would take this pupil out of his classroom for twenty minutes a day, just long enough to fill in the missing basic instruction and firm up the foundation needed to move on successfully with his group. The same approach covered cursive writing which is introduced at different times in different schools. If more than one child in a class exhibited the same or similar problems, the Child Development teacher would work with the small group almost as effectively as one-to-one.

The adaptability of the Child Development Program was demonstrated again, a few years later. In response to a suggestion made at an administrative meeting, the Child Development teachers also met daily with first graders in the lowest reading groups for a twenty-minute Reading, Review, and Reinforcement Program as a follow-up to the regular classroom reading group session. By reviewing the basic vocabulary and using those words in varied ways such as in scrambling and unscrambling, alphabetizing, making rhyming words, drawing pictures for each word, and rereading that day's portion of their classroom book, many of these insecure young readers became more confident, more skilled, and more successful, moving on to the middle and even the top reading groups within a few weeks.

It should be noted that the benefits of the Child Development Program reach out from pre-kindergarten to grade six, including ungraded classes of neurologically and/or perceptually handicapped youngsters. Some of the most dramatic improvements have been noted in an ungraded class where the Child Development teacher spent thirty-five minutes a week giving the whole group of ten children handwriting lessons.

Having been involved in the Child Development Program since 1968 (taking Martha Palmer's place), the author has been one of its strongest advocates. She hopes through the publication of this book to spread the word and good work that previously has been confined to the public schools of North Brunswick, New Jersey.

CHAPTER 13

Sources:
Where to Get What You Need to Start the Child Development Program in Your School

Every effort has been made to verify availability of the items listed below. It would still be a good idea to call (many have free "800" numbers) or write and ask for a catalog before placing an order.

Ann Arbor Tracking Materials—Academic Therapy Publications, 20 Commercial Blvd., Novato, CA 94949-6191

Auditory Familiar Sounds (139R)—SRA/McGraw-Hill, 220 East Danieldale Rd., DeSoto, TX 75115-2490

Auditory Perceptual Development Remedial Activities—Psychological and Educational Publications, Inc., 1477 Rollins Road, Burlingame, CA 94010

Auditory Perception Training–Memory (7171)—Pro-Ed, 8700 Shoal Creek Blvd., Austin, TX 78758-6897

Balance Beam (84515)—J. L. Hammett Co., 1 Hammett Place, P.O. Box 859057, Braintree, MA 02185-9057

Balls (8-1/2" rubber playground balls for bouncing) (15828)—J. L. Hammett Co., 1 Hammett Place, P.O. Box 859057, Braintree, MA 02185-9057

Bean bags—see page 236 of 1995-96 Catalog—J. L. Hammett Co., 1 Hammett Place, P.O. Box 859057, Braintree, MA 02185-9057

Beginning Connected Cursive Writing—(1307) Educators Publishing Service, Inc., 31 Smith Place, Cambridge, MA 02138-1000

Blue Readiness Book—(see Rosner Readiness Books Complete Program)

BRIGANCE K & 1 Screen—Curriculum Associates, Inc., 5 Esquire Road, North Billerica, MA 01862-2589

Crayons—Kantroll–(83853) J. L. Hammett Co., 1 Hammett Place, P.O. Box 859057, Braintree, MA 02185-9057

Color Cubes (110) and Designs in Perspective (112)—SRA/McGraw-Hill, 220 East Danieldale Rd., DeSoto, TX 75115-2490

Controlled Reader—see "Guided Reading"

Cove Reading With Phonics—SRA/McGraw-Hill, 220 East Danieldale Rd. DeSoto, TX 75115-2490

Geoboards—see page 490 of 1995-96 Catalog—J. L. Hammett Co., 1 Hammett Place, P.O. Box 859057, Braintree, MA 02185-9057

Get Ready, Get Set and Go for The Code (Primers for the Explode the Code Series) (1780,1782,1784)— Educators Publishing Service, Inc., 31 Smith Place, Cambridge, MA 02138-1000

Green Readiness Book—(see Rosner Readiness Books Complete Program)

Guided Reading—see page 10 of 1995 Catalog—Taylor Associates, 200-2 E. 2nd Street, Huntington Station, NY 11746

How to Solve Story Problems (547)—SRA/McGraw-Hill, 220 East Danieldale Rd., DeSoto, TX 75115-2490

Johnson Handwriting Program (1308)—Educators Publishing Service, Inc., 31 Smith Place, Cambridge, MA 02138-1000

Learning to Listen in the Classroom—Following Directions with Multi-Word Phrases (EI-6131)—Educational Insights, 16941 Keegan Ave., Carson, CA 90746

Listening Lotto-ry (Aud. Discr.) (EI-6159)—Educational Insights, 16941 Keegan Ave., Carson, CA 90746

Marsden ball—Dr. Richard Apell, 15 Thelbridge Street, Madison, CT 06443-3412

Metronome (Electronic)—Dr. Richard Apell, 15 Thelbridge Street, Madison, CT 06443-3412

Parquetry Blocks–Large (500) and Small (115) and Accompanying Design Cards (114) and (116, 179)— SRA/McGraw-Hill, 220 East Danieldale Rd., DeSoto, TX 75115-2490

Pegs (129), Pegboards (128), and Pegboard Designs (150)—SRA/McGraw-Hill, 220 East Danieldale Rd., DeSoto, TX 75115-2490

Pencil Grippers—Grip-Rite Grippers (60274) or Stetro Pencil Grips (50069)—J. L. Hammett Co., 1 Hammett Place, P.O. Box 859057, Braintree, MA 02185-9057

Perception + —EIRC, 606 Delsea Drive, Sewell, NJ 08080-9199 Att: Lynda Lathrop

Pick-Up Sticks (80675-Rounded tips) or (83341-Classic)—J. L. Hammett Co., 1 Hammett Place, P.O. Box 859057, Braintree, MA 02185-9057

Primary Pencils—Try-Rex No. 21(53051) for K and grade one; Try-Rex No. 23(53053) for second grade; Try-Rex No. 33(53033) for grades 3-6—J. L. Hammett Co., 1 Hammett Place, P.O. Box 859057, Braintree, MA 02185-9057

Primary Phonics—(see page 10 of 1995 catalog)—Educators Publishers Service, 31 Smith Place, Cambridge, MA 02138-1000

Railroad Chalk (extra thick) (91184) or Triple-size White (91073) or Buff (91075)—J. L. Hammett Co., 1 Hammett Place, P.O. Box 859057, Braintree, MA 02185-9057

Recipe for Reading (7370)—Pro-Ed, 8700 Shoal Creek Blvd., Austin, TX 78758-6897

Rosner Readiness Books Complete Program (7450)—Pro-Ed, 8700 Shoal Creek Blvd., Austin, TX 78758-6897

Scissors—Double Handed (185 R and 185 L) and Easy Grip (361R)—SRA/McGraw-Hill, 220 East Danieldale Rd., DeSoto, TX 75115

Sequential Picture Cards I (127)—SRA/McGraw-Hill, 220 East Danieldale Rd., DeSoto, TX 75115

Sight Word Lab (637)—SRA/McGraw-Hill, 220 East Danieldale Rd., DeSoto, TX 75115

Sound Foundations—Program I (256)—SRA/McGraw-Hill, 220 East Danieldale Rd., DeSoto, TX 75115

Steenburgen Quick Math Screening Test Level I—Academic Therapy Publications, 20 Commercial Blvd., Novato, CA 94949-6191

Stencils (clear) (137)—SRA/McGraw-Hill, 220 East Danieldale Rd., DeSoto, TX 75115

Stepping Stones—Letters–(61887)—J. L. Hammett Co., 1 Hammett Place, P.O. Box 859057 Braintree, MA 02185-9057

Structural Arithmetic—(see page 44 of 1995 Catalog)—Educators Publishing Service, 31 Smith Place, Cambridge, MA 02138-1000

Structural Reading—page 66 of 1996 catalog—SRA/McGraw-Hill, 220 East Danieldale Rd., DeSoto, TX 75115

Test of Auditory-Perceptual Skills—Morrison F. Garner, Ed.D., Pro-Ed, 8700 Shoal Creek Boulevard, Austin, TX 78757-6897

Test of Visual-Motor Skills—Psychological and Educational Publications, Inc., 1477 Rollins Road, Burlingame, CA 94010

Test of Visual-Perceptual Skills (non-motor)—(ages 4-12)—Morrison F. Gardner, Ed.D., Academic Therapy Publications, 20 Commercial Blvd., Novato, CA 94949-6191

Try-Rex pencils—see "Primary Pencils"

Visual Memory Cards—Objects (181B) and Shapes (182)—SRA/McGraw-Hill, P.O. Box 543, Blacklick, OH 43004-0543

Visual Sequential Memory Exercises (284)—SRA/McGraw-Hill, P.O. Box 543, Blacklick, OH 43004-0543

Vu-Mate Tachistoscope and accompanying books—see pages 20-21 of 1995 Catalog—Taylor Associates, 200-2 E. 2nd Street, Huntington Station, NY 11746

Zaner-Bloser Red Base-Line Paper—grades K through 4—and blue and red chalks—Zaner-Bloser Educational Publishers, 2200 W. Fifth Ave., P.O. Box 16764, Columbus, OH 43216-6764

CHAPTER 14

Additional Suggested Readings

Ames, Louise Bates, *Is your Child in the Wrong Grade?* Modern Learning Press, Rosemont, NJ 08556, 1978.

Ames, Louise Bates, Gillespie, Clyde and Streff, John, *Stop School Failure,* Harper & Row, New York, 1972.

Ames, Louise Bates, Ph.D. and Chase, Joan Ames, Ph.D., *Don't Push Your Preschooler,* Harper & Row, New York, 1974.

Cohen, Neville S., O.D., and Shapiro, Joseph L., O.D., *Out of Sight Into Vision,* Simon and Schuster, New York, 1977.

Edelman, Ellis S., *The Suddenly Successful Student,* Sutter House, P.O. Box 212, Lititz, PA 17543, 1986.

Flach, Frederic, M.D., *Rickie,* Ballantine Books, New York, 1990.

Furth, Hans G. and Wachs, Harry, *Thinking Goes to School,* Oxford University Press, New York, 1976.

Harmon, Darell Boyd, *Dynamic Theory of Vision,* self-published, Austin, Texas, 1958.

Ilg, Frances L. and Ames, Louise Bates, *School Readiness,* Harper & Row, New York, 1964.

Kavner, Richard S., O.D. *Your Children's Vision,* Simon & Schuster, New York, 1986.

Kavner, Richard S., O.D. and Dusky, Lorraine, *Total Vision,* A. & W. Publishers, Inc., New York, 1978.

Kirshner, A. J., *Training That Makes Sense,* Academic Therapy Publications, Novato, California, 1972.

Levy, H. *Square Pegs, Round Holes,* Little, Brown and Company, New York, 1973.

Liberman, Jacob, O.D., Ph.D., *Light: Medicine of the Future,* Bear & Co., Inc. Santa Fe, New Mexico, 1991.

Radler, D. H. and Kephart, Newell C., *Success Through Play,* Harper & Bros., New York, 1960.

Rosner, Jerome, *Helping Children Overcome Learning Difficulties,* Walker & Co., New York, 1975.

Seiderman, Dr. Arthur S., Marcus, Dr. Steven E., and Hapgood, David, *20/20 is Not Enough,* Ballantine Books, New York, 1991.

Wiener, Harold, O.D., *Eyes OK, I'm OK,* Academic Therapy Publications, Novato, California, 1977.

Wunderlich, Ray, *Kids, Brains and Learning,* Johnny Reads, Inc., St. Petersburg, Florida, 1970.

Young, Milton A. *Teaching Children with Special Learning Needs: A Problem-Solving Approach,* John Day Company, New York, 1967.

Index